REVELATIONS

FOR A NEW ERA

Keys to Restoring Paradise on Earth

Revised Edition

A Matthew Book with Suzanne Ward

ISBN 978-0-9717875-2-0

Library of Congress 2002090383

MATTHEW BOOKS
P. O. Box 1043
Camas, Washington 98607

www.matthewbooks.com
suzy@matthewbooks.com

Printed in the United States of America

Cover redesigned by Hartmut Jager

READERS' COMMENTS

Revelations for a New Era, a synthesis of vital knowledge that it would take 100 other books to disclose, satisfies the seeker of truth and spiritual knowledge like no other book I have ever read.

Russ Michael, *Finding your Soulmate*, Austria

Revelations for a New Era is a treasure trove of priceless information for humankind. It gives unprecedented instruction for happy and successful living in the world today and is an invaluable guideline for all who seek deeper understanding of the vast and constant changes we continue to experience on all levels of our lives.

Iris Freelander, D.D., California

This book relays a great deal of fascinating and extremely relevant information about our soul's journey of evolution and is a guideline as we prepare for the shift in planetary consciousness. I consider the Matthew Books to be some of the most important writings on the planet today.

Kiara Windrider, *Doorway to Eternity*, India

Revelations for a New Era is one of the most uplifting, inspiring and spiritually educational books you will ever read. It will answer any questions on spiritual topics you could pose, as well as give insight into what is happening today on the planet and in the etheric waves surrounding it.

**Chris Hamilton,
On the Path to Enlightenment, Australia**

REVELATIONS
FOR A NEW ERA

CONTENTS

PART I   OUR COSMIC HERITAGE

PART II   UNIVERSAL ENERGY

PART III   OUR SOUL CONNECTION

PART IV   CREATION

PART V   VIEWS OF EARTH AND OTHER WORLDS

PART VI   UNIVERSAL BROTHERHOOD

Part VII   CREATOR'S DECREE

PART VIII   CONTROVERSIES

PART IX   A SPIRITUAL RESPONSE
TO TERRORISM

PART X   2012

FOREWORD

This revision came about in 2008 because the publisher of the French edition requested updated information wherever applicable and the translator asked for simplified wording wherever possible. Throughout the revision process I worked with Matthew and the other sources of the original material, and all were delighted with the results of our cooperative efforts. So, when the inventory of the first revised edition—published specifically to include Part IX, "A Spiritual Response to Terrorism"—neared depletion, we ordered this updated version that also is being published in Japanese and translated for a Spanish edition.

The beginning of the original book was early 1994, when my telepathic connection opened with my son Matthew, almost 14 years after his death at age 17 in 1980. However, within the universal time/space continuum, the genesis of this material is—well, literally timeless. It was arranged before Matthew's birth, before my birth and his father's, before the birth of our parents and their parents, ad infinitum. Our minds cannot comprehend happenings outside our linear time structure of past, present and future; and as Matthew told me, even in the continuum, the matching up of these many souls and their simultaneous relationships is a complex undertaking. But all of the genetic and environmental influences of our lineage extending back to antiquity were necessary for Matthew and me to become exactly who we needed to be at this point in our souls' journey, collaborators in an unusual Heaven and Earth venture.

Of course, I had no idea of this when our telepathic

communion started. Sittings, as I call our daily conversations that I record on the computer, were a source of joy
and wonderment as I received astonishing information
from him and the beings he introduced to me. But I soon
learned that this had a far more important purpose.
Matthew told me that a provision of our family's pre-birth
agreement was my work as a journal editor and writer
because I would need that experience to prepare for
publication the messages that he and many others were
transmitting to me.

I was accustomed to working with authors on
Earth—eliminating verbosity and redundancy and doing
other polishing while preserving the integrity of the information and the personality of the writer—but editing the
words of "celestial authors" was intimidating. However,
once underway I felt a strong sense of the divine guidance
Matthew had promised and I was at ease working with all
the sources whose messages are in this book.

Acting upon God's mandate, the Council of Nirvana
(the governing body of the realm we call Heaven) invited
representatives of other civilizations to send messages to
the people of Earth. Other sources volunteered and were
approved by the Council. All of the presentations have
the same theme—*We have come in love and friendship
to enlighten, advise and assist you and your planet*—but
the descriptions of their civilizations, homelands and
history are fascinatingly different. Although I wasn't
interviewing those vast, powerful entities whose massive
energy and intelligence is beyond my imagining, I had
questions that led into new avenues of astonishing
information. If I eliminated my part there would be no
logical continuation of their messages, so in most cases,
what were intended to be formal presentations evolved
into conversations.

Residents of Nirvana and members of the other civilizations represented in this book can speak audibly, but telepathy is their usual form of communication and always it is the mode of extraterrestrial communication with Earth. Not only do other civilizations study Earth languages, but they can clearly understand all communication methods in the universe through a process that translates all thoughts into a single universal language, "the language of light."

Other-world sources never invade the privacy of our thoughts and feelings; however, they are instantly connected with us via the energy of our thoughts and feelings about them. That's why Matthew and the others can answer questions in my mind and comment on my emotional reaction to what they are saying. And, I "hear" voices in ordinary conversational pace and tones with differing sounds and inflections, just as we are accustomed to hearing and speaking.

You may wonder why Matthew sometimes speaks casually and at other times quite formally, often within the same conversation. The difference is due to the makeup of the soul. Matthew is an independent and inviolate part of a larger soul entity that he calls his "cumulative soul." He refers to his lifetime as my son as his "personage," which is only one aspect of his larger soul entity that includes many personages, and each has full knowledge of all the others' lifetime experiencing. Whereas he and all other souls at his stage of evolution have the composite knowledge of their respective cumulative souls available, like a handy reference library, we have no conscious knowledge of our own "soul relatives" or their lifetimes. (This relationship is explained in the chapters, "The Soul" and "The Cumulative Soul," PART III.)

Matthew speaks in accordance with my feelings and thoughts. When those are personal in nature, his personage is predominant because my energy vibrations are evoking that aspect, and then he speaks in a natural way for any mother-and-son discussion. When my interests are more academic, his cumulative soul automatically responds to that difference in my vibrations and then he sounds like a professor giving a lecture.

The timeless information in Parts I-IV and VI and scattered throughout other sections of the book was transmitted between March and August 1994. In this revised edition, some information that was timely years ago, while still interesting, was eliminated and two lengthy presentations were condensed to make space for new material. Selected chapters in Parts V and VIII, which were transmitted at various times from 1994 until early 2003, were updated in 2008 to include the most current information at that time on those topics. In that same vein, some relevant short excerpts from later books or paraphrased parts of Matthew's messages posted on www.matthewbooks.com are integrated into the original material. During my review of this revision just prior to printing, Matthew asked me to insert his paraphrasing of comments in his recent messages about the swine flu "pandemic."

When he transmitted the original material, he was living in Nirvana, the proper name of the spirit world we call Heaven, and many of his statements include "here" in referring to that world. In 1998 he was given the choice of becoming a member of the 100-member Council of Nirvana, incarnating in a highly advanced civilization, or accepting the invitation of physical populations to assist them in upgrading their spirit realms. He chose the last, and since then has been traveling, astrally or in spacecraft, throughout this galaxy and others, and he manifests a body that fits in with the civilization he is visiting. This also gives him a higher vantage point for reporting current happenings on Earth.

Information on the Internet (and more recently, occasionally in mainstream media) confirms what Matthew told me well before its emergence in those sources. For example, his explanation in 1994 of energy's physical, mental and emotional effects on us is especially obvious in the proliferation of prescription drugs for a large variety of more recent diagnoses, including ADD, ADHD and depression. Clinical research has uncovered and reported the dangers of vaccines and inoculations, including claims that they are responsible for the huge increase in cases of autism—Matthew spoke about this over ten years ago. The manmade weather control technology he mentioned soon after our telepathic connection opened over fifteen years ago has become public knowledge, and evidence amassed by scientists and other researchers about the terrorism of September 11, 2001, substantiates what he told me right after "9/11" (Part IX).

Often Matthew uses masculine pronouns to denote both male and female. As he requested of me, *"Please accept this as intended, only for ease of my speaking and your hearing and NEVER as a suggestion of male priority in any respect."*

Reading the glossary now could be helpful as the meaning of some terms differs from our standard definitions.

Suzanne Ward
July 2009

PART I

OUR COSMIC HERITAGE

HIERARCHY OF CREATOR

MATTHEW: To understand the purpose of our lives, there must be an understanding of our relationship with Creator, the ultimate power in the cosmos. It is a relationship as simply stated as the father and his children, but the origin of our souls within Creator cannot be stated that easily.

The energy of Creator/Creation—the proper designation of the Totality or Source or Oneness of All—is pure love-light and it is the most powerful force in the cosmos. That name designation also is the most descriptive, encompassing both the total essence of that ultimate source and the creative action. For simplicity in communication, we usually say only Creator.

There was nothing before Creator and nothing except the sleeping power of Creator until Its first self-expression of Its essence. In that moment, which some call the "Big Bang," the original fragmentation of Creator's love and wisdom and power came forth as individual soul entities. The term "fragmentation" in this context is not a severing or a breaking down of the whole; it is bestowing upon all the individual parts the same properties, or elements, that make up the whole. And from that first instant of Creation, those first souls and everything else that exists throughout the cosmos are inseparable from Creator and each other. At soul level, ALL IS ONE and forevermore shall be.

However irreverent this analogy may seem, it is the best visual aid I can think of, so I ask you to imagine the spiritual hierarchy of Creator as a pie. The entire pie is

Creator Soul: the Omnipotent Totality, the Source of All; and at the center is Creator Mind: Omniscience, All Knowledge. Starting at the center, imagine a series of concentric rings superimposed over the whole pie—the rings are the spheres of the hierarchy, the flexible divisions of Creator.

The visual aid now requires an unusual perspective for accurate representation. Imagine the pie cut into countless slices whose widest ends touch the center, the limitless mind of Creator, and become narrower as the slices enter rings successively farther from the midpoint. The slivers represent the independently experiencing soul fragments of Creator that have been created, or manifested, throughout all time. Every portion contains *proportionally* exactly the same ingredients as the total pie and no portion is separate from another. It is the same throughout All of Creation.

Now we return to the Beginning, when Creator first divided Itself. Each of the fragments within that first sphere of the spiritual hierarchy's perfect light and purity had the identical powers of Creator. This is the sphere of Christed light, where the paternal power called Archangel Michael and the other archangels originated, and where for unknown eons only pure awareness existed. Then Creator gave to all those parts of Itself the ultimate gift, free will with its inherent power of co-creating ability— "co-creating" because the energy source for producing anything comes from Creator and the productions come from the ideas of the souls. And so it was that those highest angels and Creator made the second angelic sphere. Although not as close to Creator Mind as the archangels, these newer souls also were composed of pure light, without form or substance.

After reflection for untold ages, the two angelic

realms had the idea to co-create souls with life form *potential*—they had the choice of remaining discarnate, without form, or manifesting a form for wider experiencing. The co-creations in this third sphere are the celestial bodies throughout the universes and the gods and goddesses, who could choose to remain discarnate or embody in male or female forms—either way, these souls are androgynous, the perfect balance of male and female energies. As we understand it, the souls Creator selected to reign over the universes are discarnate. They may show their presence as near-blinding golden white light, but their unlimited co-creating powers and ideas are evident in everything that exists within their respective universes.

One of those gods is the Supreme Being of our universe and, with Creator, created everything within it. Since our god is called God by some Earth religions and that is how you think of Him, Mother, that is how I shall refer to Him. Also, God is a perfect blend of male and female energies and Mother/Father God accurately expresses His essence, but on Earth He usually is referred to only as Father and with masculine pronouns. That evolved naturally when male energies began to dominate the nature of Earth civilizations millennia back in your timing; and even though feminine, or goddess, energy is being beamed to the planet in abundance, simply for ease of speaking I shall use the more usual masculine designations you are accustomed to.

Now then, for ever-greater experiencing, God's original beings, which are called root souls, expressed themselves into divisions called soul fragments or soul sparks, or God fragments or God sparks. Similarly and successively, those souls divided themselves into sparklets, who divided themselves into sub-sparklets.

Entities created by further fragmentation also are called sub-sparklets. The myriad individual, independent and inviolate lifetimes of every soul at all levels of fragmentation are called "personages."

I gave you those designations—and there may be others too—only to show the *order of lineage* in the innumerable spheres radiating outward from the mind of Creator. None of the designations defines the souls' *spiritual evolution* status, and simply "soul" is sufficient because there is no difference in each one's connection with Creator or its makeup in proportional measure. ALWAYS the life force of even the newest soul is its own independent, inviolate Self, and it is connected inseparably to God and Creator, just as every single cell in your body is both a viable, independently functioning cell and at the same time is an inseparable aspect of the composite—the person you are.

S: Matthew, where does our current population fit into the subdivided spheres?

MATTHEW: Primarily at sub-sparklet level, but remember, Mother, that's NOT soul *evolution*—it's only the order the personage souls emerged for independent experiencing! I think your expression "old soul" pertains to the evolution part and not the order of lineage. Those may have nothing at all to do with each other, because spiritual growth is determined by each soul's free will choices and not how many lifetimes it took to make the choices that elevated it to a higher level of spiritual evolution. And now—a time that is without precedence not only on Earth but in the universe!—there are some extremely "old souls" on your planet to guide the rest of you to greater enlightenment.

S: Oh, I see. Thank you, dear. Is Creator the supreme being of the cosmos and God is an assistant?

MATTHEW: No. Cosmos and universe often are used interchangeably as synonymous terms, but each universe is only one part of the cosmos, which has several universes, and each has its own god or goddess as its Supreme Being. Because people on Earth are not aware of other universes and their rulers or the spiritual creation hierarchy, God is the name some religions have given to Creator. This is using a generic term for a formal name, like naming a baby girl Girl. And it is not uncommon or incorrect for God to be referred to as "our creator," because He *is*, but that adds just another element of confusion about Creator and God and the names.

I don't know how the name error started. It may have been some deviation of reference in deepest antiquity, when it was known that Creator/Creation is the Source, All That Is, I AM, Almighty, Oneness, Totality or other name to denote Creator as Supreme Being of the entire cosmos. The name doesn't matter. When love and reverence are given to Creator in name and to God in meaning or vice versa, the communion is honored in fullness.

The Trinity of the Christian churches could be interpreted like this: Father (Creator: the highest power in the cosmos, who is called God or other names in your religions). Son (God, who is the creation, or the "son" of Creator, and although the Supreme Being only of our universe, is not generally recognized on Earth as different from Creator). Holy Ghost (the realm, or sphere closest to Creator, also called the Christed realm, where the highest beings are total love expressed as light; and from whence come the souls who incarnate to become major spiritual influences throughout this universe, including Jesus the Christ and Buddha the Christ on Earth).

Regardless of the difference in names and interpretations, the interconnectedness of this triune order is the same. And there is no difference in the divine order of the Almighty Omnipotent and Omniscient Creator Being and Its subsequent powers, only in the names as they have evolved.

GOD

S: Do God and Creator differ in any way besides the size of their "jurisdiction"?

MATTHEW: Yes, there are two essential differences, but first let me repeat that any part of Creator contains ALL of Its elements. Therefore, God is a perfect, undiluted expression of Creator and *in effect* is Creator for this universe—Creator mind in knowledge and wisdom, Creator heart in love, Creator power in authority and responsibility.

Now, the first essential difference is this: Creator's core essence is the center of order and life in the cosmos, and a vital function of that essence is not active. Like the axle of a wheel provides an "anchor" for the parts in motion, the stable force within Creator enables the constant motion of Its other parts. If that stability ceased, life itself would cease. The creation of life in any form requires the measured pace of energy frequencies, and that requires both the stable and the active aspects of Creator's functioning.

God is active in all aspects. As the magnified active force of Creator in this universe, with the same quality and extent of Creator's love and light energy essence, God initiates all life forms and all order here. Just as in the cosmos where the highest, most powerful energy is light—the essence of Creator—so is that true in this universe—the essence of God. Light is a fluctuating, expanding and contracting motion ever increasing in its power to encompass more loving capacity and sensation. Light can be directed but never captured or destroyed, and Love is infinite. This love-light force, which is the same energy simply expressed differently, is the foundation of individual souls interacting with God.

Because life in all forms in our universe comes from God, it can be said that humans are made in His image by attributing to Him His human creations. The idea of a human appearance and the material of which physical bodies are made came from the mind of God.

With the creation of life in our universe He set in motion the unstoppable momentum of laws that govern everything from the orbiting of galaxies to a seed knowing when to emerge from its covering and start growing. For the immeasurable time since this was started, only the refinements of energy direction through technology have changed the original course of energy's divine purpose and motion. There cannot be any change within energy itself because energy IS creation. It is how energy is tapped into and used that is the key to creating.

In the beginning, all creation within this universe was flawless, pure, holy and loving. All was in perfect harmony and union, and life was meant to be lived like that. Creator intended free will to be a gift to all souls— that is why, by cosmic law, rulers of all the universes are bound to honor the free will choices of every soul in their respective domains. But it is possible that this Gift of all gifts, the total freedom of souls to choose, has been so abused and misused that it cannot be regarded as the golden gift it once was. In some universes free will is unknown, so we are told, and even in parts of this universe, souls have absorbed the gift into such radiance that it no longer is an individual decision, but rather a unified choice of myriad collective souls. However, in accordance with Creator's law, on Earth free will is the order of life wherein the hand of God is ever-present in observation but never permitted to restrict or deny souls' choices.

The second essential difference between Creator and God is this: Whereas Creator is aware of each individual life throughout the cosmos, there is no standard for Its involvement in the lives of the souls or interaction with them. God is not only aware of each soul's station in this universe, He knows every person's heartaches, secret dreams, torments, joys, fears. ALL is known to God.

When Creator left Its state of sublime stillness, the purpose was to experience through creating. As the perfect expression of Creator, God has the same purpose, and Ilis sentient aspect is within every one of His creations in any incarnate or discarnate lifetime. He feels the very same emotions being felt by all souls in spirit or in physical worlds. Not for even one instant is He detached from the total sensations of all souls regardless of their spiritual evolvement status and free will choices, and this also pertains to *every* life form within the animal and plant kingdoms.

At a much higher level, God experiences the anguish of Earth in her present turmoil and heavy negativity, and the sensations of every other celestial body as well. I cannot state too often the inseparability of God from *every* life form in His universe, and that same interconnectedness is true of each soul with every other soul in all life forms. The term "personal God" that sometimes is used on Earth is absolutely accurate because God IS every person there as well as every other soul in the animal and plant kingdoms. Feeling the collective sensations of all life on Earth, much less the sensations of ALL life throughout this universe, simultaneously is impossible for even the most highly evolved souls in this universe to imagine.

S: Since Creator doesn't become involved in our lives, does that mean It (?!) doesn't feel souls' physical pain and emotional suffering like God does?

MATTHEW: Mother, "It" as a pronoun for Creator is not demeaning. This use cannot be compared with your "it" indicating a thing or condition rather than a being. When applied to Creator, It is akin to white: White is not devoid of color, it is the color composite. From white, all colors of the universe are refracted into their own essences, and elsewhere in the universe are many magnificent hues unknown on your planet.

Now then, Creator does indeed experience feelings of souls throughout Creation, and to a far vaster height of sentience than the capacity of your third density bodies, but It does not become involved or give personal response to any soul's situation. God, on the other hand, constantly has in motion all avenues of potential assistance for His souls within their pre-birth agreement choices. The arms of God, if you will, embrace each and every soul in this universe, and faster than the blink of an eye, his emissaries respond to his authorizing their aid to souls in distress that is not in their agreements.

UNIVERSES

S: From your vantage point, how would you describe our universe and the others?

MATTHEW: In one respect we see our universe the same as your science describes it. We see the entirety of all galaxies with their suns, planets, asteroids, moons, comets, and rings of gaseous materials and debris within the parameters of this universe. Not to God and Creator, but to us, the number of celestial bodies is truly countless. We also see all bodies and their movement within the flexible boundaries as the "universal mass" and all intelligence everywhere as the "universal mind."

There is a constantly moving order to all the universes as if to keep themselves clean through the motion, like water running and purifying itself. The constant motion is expansion and contraction, and distances are not as much affected as the intensity of the energy forces.

Experiencing life in our universe is in accordance with the Beginnings when God created the human—(H)igher (U)niversal MAN—family, but we can only assume that other universes are for similar experiencing. That is not within our knowledge at this level of understanding the divine mystery of the cosmos.

Although the number of universes cannot be ascertained here because of the fluidity of motion wherein the boundaries can be dissolved as one universal mind melds with another, the current number is thought to be seven. We are told the coalescing can happen only harmoniously, never by conquering. The light emanating from the union of two universal minds is mistakenly interpreted by your science as the collision of two large celestial bodies or the implosion of a star.

We have another definition of universe: any progressive learning area of the universal mind that a soul enters to continue its evolution. There are growth stages that require moving into a placement so different from familiar ones that it is an entirely new level of experiencing, and in this sense the number of universes is boundless. Also in this sense, what you call "black holes" are entryways for souls into new learning and "white holes" are exits— you go into blackness with no knowledge of what is there and you exit enLIGHTened because you have completed the learning that space offers.

PART II

UNIVERSAL ENERGY

ENERGY, ENERGY ATTACHMENTS

MATTHEW: Everything in the universe starts and continues with energy, and nothing exists or happens without energy motion. Energy is neutral; energy attachments are positive or negative. For simplicity in speaking, often we drop the word "attachments" and refer to energy by the intent of its usage or the qualification its attachments impart, such as "light" energy or "dark," or "positive" energy or "negative," or negativity or positivity.

Creator is the only source of energy, but there are countless sources of energy attachments—*everything that has ever been created!* I shall explain this in the context of what is happening on Earth right now. The sound and fury in the heavens signifies that negative entities are trying to kill your planet. When the energy behind the sounds accumulates sufficiently to cause motion, natural disasters happen. Those have their own sounds, which feed into the accumulated sound "pit," and this further feeds a momentum that cannot be stopped, only played out until spent.

At this time in Earth's evolution she must relieve herself of pressures caused by negative attachments. Some have been created by Earth humankind who knowingly and willfully caused and still are causing death, misery, sorrow, hardship and destruction to life in all its forms, and some have been created by off-planet beings that have the same intent. Both the intentional actions and the resultant suffering create negativity, and under this heavy influence, energy is forcing itself down upon the planet.

Negativity in deeper pockets and in higher atmospheres also is having a considerable effect upon the energy near Earth's surface. Once the momentum has been built to the force level of eruption, there is activity on the scale needed to relieve the pressure just above and beneath the planet's surface. Volcanic eruptions, earthquakes and violent storms are Earth's natural ways to do that. Once the energy behind those natural disasters has dissipated, it is again completely neutral because it is free of influence. It enters an equally neutral universal pool of energy where it is available for the cycle to start again.

The "play" of energy is as neutral as energy itself. What gives energy its negative or positive attachments are the thought forms created by those intent-and-result sources or Earth's residents' interpretations of events. For instance, when rain causes flooding and widespread damage, the reaction to the rain is with negative feelings. Once set in motion as thought waves, the vibrations of those feelings attract similar forces that then join the common pool of negativity on Earth. During a drought, rain is greeted with thankfulness, and this positive reaction adds to the positive energy pool. Thus the opposing forces of energy are built.

Not all of the collective energy affecting Earth derives from weather events. That is a large part of energy activity during the past few decades, but it is the *result*, not the cause of the abundance of energy swirling within and around Earth. The countless thought forms that started erratic weather patterns are the greater source and cause of that energy movement.

Although all thought forms are universally inter-connected, every thought, regardless of how insignificant you may consider it, has its own existence. Thought forms created by people on Earth most affect the planet because they are the ones closest to you; however, you use only a small portion of your brain power, so your thought forms are correspondingly small in range. They are only a fraction as powerful as those originating from beings in other placements where brain power has been developed to a far greater percentage of its potential than it has among people on Earth. The energy from the thought forms of those more powerful sources reaches Earth and mingles with the energy already accumulated there.

S: *How does the energy of those distant sources reach here?*

MATTHEW: You **invite** it! LIKE ATTRACTS LIKE! Forces are at work in the universe that are "for" or "against" the good of Earth. The thought forms you originate attract like thought forms from the far greater brain power of the distant entities. By universal law you must invite them to come, and they are indeed being invited! Your INTENT is the basis of that invitation. Intent has the greatest impact upon you and the planet because out of intent come the thought forms. Whether your intent is "good" or "bad," it is your invitation to like-minded or like-intentioned entities to join and energize with yourself.

In this way, negativity begets negativity, and its effects are seen everywhere on Earth! Thought forms *never* can be destroyed and they never disintegrate, and negative thought forms are like shards of glass or jagged concrete. Imagine Earth's atmosphere filled with those propelled chunks of glass and concrete and what they can do to ALL life on the planet! The negative thought forms are having exactly that destructive effect!

You attribute pollution to toxic waste or fumes, acid rain, smog and so forth, but those are the results of negativity. It is NEGATIVITY that forms the pollutants and creates their damaging aspects! With the healing effects of positive thought forms in unconditional love, the damaging effects of the negative thought forms can be soothed and ultimately healed. And that's the ONLY way! LOVE replacing all the negative thoughts and feelings is the ONLY way this can come about!

Mother, this is a very emotional subject for me, and my message has become quite disjointed. Please remedy it. Our words are no more sacred than you consider your own. However, our information...

(HATONN) ...PUT THIS IN CAPS, SUZANNE...

S: Hatonn?

HATONN: YES! OUR INFORMATION IS SACRED...

MATTHEW: ...but we know better than to think a poorly expressed presentation must be preserved intact just because it originated on this side.

S: Matthew, did you know that Hatonn interrupted you? I didn't just imagine that he spoke some of the words in your statement, did I?

MATTHEW: No, Mother, you didn't imagine it. That was Hatonn. His energy is unmistakable, as you know. Since he is the principal master of information passing from here to there, and apparently he felt I needed to emphasize more strongly the importance of that message to people on Earth, it was his prerogative to interrupt.

THOUGHT FORMS

MATTHEW: Good morning, Mother—your energy is wonderful! When you are as enthusiastic as you are today, the flow is like a rushing river, singing and overflowing with excitement at its new course of expansion. In light of your receptivity to energy other than mine, would you like Imaca to come, at least to say "Hello"?

S: *Yes, I would.*

MATTHEW: He is here, in response to my energy beep.

S: *Good morning, Imaca. Welcome back.*

IMACA: I welcome you in the returning to me, Miss Suzy. It has been a while since we spoke and exchanged thoughts. I congratulate you on your progress. I enjoy being back in your energy field, which is soft and with the sensation of welcoming my thought impressions into your consciousness.

Would you like to have a substantive discussion or would you prefer to wait until tomorrow? I see your preference for tomorrow. And now I see your question about my use of "see" in that context. A thought can be seen because it has a substantial form and it pulses, which catches our attention. Instantly there is cognitive recognition of your thinking intent, but the thought form itself literally is seen.

S: *Is only my brain involved or is it something inherent in the soul itself?*

IMACA: This mental activity is the province of the soul using the brain as the instrument in the same way you use a computer to record your desired words. The brain is only a tool. It is like your computer that does not operate by itself, but only when you interact with it, and then it performs for you. The soul and the brain have the same relationship of activity. The soul "turns on" the brain, which then stimulates soul depth knowledge and puts it into useful action within the mind.

Knowledge is not within the brain except as it is entered by the soul, and then it is used by the mind for reasoning. The knowledge is accumulated, but it is not as easily accessed in the current lifetimes on Earth as in many former periods of the planet's history. The barriers imposed long, long ago by negatively-intentioned entities have been successful in hiding most of the information from your conscious knowing.

S: Thank you for explaining that, Imaca.

IMACA: You are most welcome, Miss Suzy. As it developed, I did have worthwhile information to impart by virtue of your questions. For your service in receiving, I thank you. And I shall say "farewell" to you in love and light, as Matthew awaits the pleasure of your company.

S: I'm glad you came today, Imaca—thank you. Matthew, hello again. I tried to follow what Imaca was saying, but "seeing thoughts" is beyond my comprehension. I suppose you see my thoughts, too.

MATTHEW: I see your thoughts as easily as I know your heart, Mother. Both your thoughts and your feelings produce forms of indelible nature. I am aware of them by being *within* them, but only to the extent that I am invited. The invitation is registered by the intensity of your emotions and thoughts that include me.

S: Well dear, don't you ever wonder if you're wrong in what you think my thoughts are?

MATTHEW: It never occurred to me to wonder about this! Mother, there is no gap between your thoughts or your words typed on this computer or your spoken words and my awareness of them *when you wish*. Either I have no knowledge because I am not invited or I have accurate knowledge because I am. Never is there "intrusion," only entry upon invitation! There are no barriers between your energy system and mine when you want our communion in any form.

S: How can you be sure it's my energy and not someone else's?

MATTHEW: I cannot mistake your energy, and not only because it's so close to my own vibratory rate. Your energy is unique to you. I pick up your signals whether or not you're consciously aiming them at me, such as in our conversations. When you are thinking of me, that thought form becomes a vibration, and its pulsing tone distinguishes it from all other tones in the universe.

To explain how I separate your sound from all the others, let us say that sounds—energy pulses, or tones— are assigned numerical rates on a tonal scale from 1 to 1000. Between the numbers are side exits for changes in the pitch or frequency as the messages and thoughts are sorted, ranked and distributed. On this very flexible numerical scale are grooves that allow the various wavelengths, or sounds that the thought forms turn into, to fall into place for identification purposes.

These identical processes, which are instantaneous and accurate, apply to everyone. I can tell whether the tones are yours, Eric's, Betsy's, Michael's and so forth. I *feel* them rather than having to go check them, like your looking into a mailbox to see if anything has arrived.

Also Mother, the love in your thought forms reaches me intact. It is a beautiful sound with a tinkling sensation and a tinkling vibration. It's truly charming and so welcome not only to me, but throughout this realm.

S: That's a lovely thought for me to have, Matthew, and for you to see. Both you and Imaca have used the term "thought forms," and I don't really understand what those are. Please give me a simple explanation.

MATTHEW: Very well, Mother. Energy and thought forms are the basis of all life and thought forms are the eternal stuff of universal knowledge. Understanding this in the universal sense is essential for comprehending the essence of ourselves.

Everything that exists throughout the universe has been created by a thought form, and energy is the building material. Thought forms "harness" energy in an amount necessary to form a dense being or object. Your body is a thought form, Mother. It originated in the universal consciousness prior to your birth, in the agreement process that involved your parents, their parents and so on, as well as our own family and your closest friends of this lifetime. Thought forms precede the germination and gestation processes of every life.

The materials that form your body are pulsing continuously with energy motion. If this were not so, your physical life would end. It is motion that sustains life, not a pumping heart or a brain wave, but energy in motion. The motion of your body breathing is apparent, but it is no more real than the motion of the atoms that compose that lamp beside you, whose movement is at a frequency not apparent to your vision. Both of these two greatly different types of existence originated with a thought form.

As you've heard, there are both negative and positive thought forms. Negative thought forms are not destroyed or neutralized by positive thought forms. Love is the synthesis of all life in the spiritual path. Love absorbs balanced entities and it can influence, or neutralize, negative ones, but it cannot annihilate them. Neutralization is not a combustion type of action, but rather a softening influence that is made available, and a negative thought form may or may not respond to that influence and balance itself.

Mother, you are groping for understanding, and no wonder. You requested a simple explanation, and mine wasn't. This would be a good time for you to receive the formal presentation Ithaca offers to everyone here who wants this information, just as you do.

Her energy is here now. It connected with mine instantly, as I thought of her with strong intent. So, what do you say?

S: I say, "Thank you!" Hello, Ithaca. Thank you for coming to my aid.

ITHACA: Good morning, dear soul. I am pleased to greet you again, especially in this helpful fashion. It is joyous for me to be within your energy that is so receptive to my own. Please understand that I have no more knowledge than Matthew, only more occasions on which I have talked about thought forms and thus have more practice. Shall I begin?

S: Yes, please.

ITHACA: Thought forms are nebulous substances in the absoluteness of a thought itself, and all activity is born of these forms. They are available infinitely and eternally to whoever wishes to contact them. The substance of thought forms is plasma, which is beyond the particles of energy that have been identified by Earth scientists. The plasma has its own density, with a stickiness quality that is directly attracted to a matching thinking and imaging thought form substance.

Inspiration connects a thinking, searching person with the existing thought form that matches the search topic. For instance, a scientist wishes to design a "small thing" that will provide light. His thought form is hazy, only the idea that something could be made for that purpose, but with no image of what that might be. His idea of a "small thing with light" connects with the light bulb form already existing in the universal pool of knowledge. When the scientist's mind connects with the image of the bulb, he calls this connection "inspiration."

In the order of the process happenings, it started with a thought form the scientist does not know already exists in the universal knowledge pool. Next came the scientist's own thought form in hazy shape but with the desire and intent to produce light from a "small thing." Then came the connection of these two thought forms, which were attracted to each other by their matching likeness. Then came the image of a light bulb shape, which the scientist thinks is solely his idea.

S: Thank you, Ithaca. That was a wonderful way to describe a thought form in action. Would you please give me an example of a more commonplace occurrence than a scientific discovery.

ITHACA: I shall be happy to do this. Please imagine that you are passing a shop and you see through the window a vibrant flower with orange petals, a brown center and shiny green leaves. When you see this flower, does the image come to you first and afterwards, the descriptive words and the name of the flower, if known to you, are crystallized in your mind?

S: Well, it seems to be simultaneous.

ITHACA: The imaging process happens so swiftly that you are unaware of a series of events that transpires between your first sight of the flower and your recognition of it as such. When you first see it, your visual thought form shoots out toward the sticky mass of thought forms throughout the universe, where the matching thought form that identifies it as a flower is accessed. The two thought forms instantly adhere to each other, and the resulting image, which you then recognize as a specific flower, registers in your brain.

If you did not know the name of the flower, your thought form would contain only a pleasant sensation and photographic realization of a flower with orange petals and brown center and green leaves. Sensory correlation is the sensation of pleasure that is registered, seemingly simultaneously. However, it was the image registered in your thought form in combination with the universe's matching thought form that produced your recognition of the vision of the flower.

S: How would a blind person function in any recognition connection? There's no vision to start the process.

ITHACA: A good observation. We have no vision limitation here, but now I see that vision is not the most appropriate word to use in this explanation. Imaging is more correct. Someone who has no sight still has imaging ability. The image is registered in the area of the brain that sends out a lightning-fast request for understanding, or description. Sometimes this has a word recognition thought form connection as well as an imaging recognition thought form.

Let us suppose that a blind person touches a flower. Even without the sight of it, a mental image is formed. The mental recognition process of an object or condition or situation combined with the sensory, or emotional correlation process, produces a thought form with "edges." The edges can act like puzzle pieces, each fitting into only one place in the entire picture. When the fit is made, both processes are set in motion toward the whole. All the steps from the first awareness of the object, condition or situation through mental recognition and sensory realization are with such speed that you never are aware of a delay in comprehension. This process for a blind person is the same as for one who has sight.

There are other aspects to thought form compliance within the universal knowledge realm, to be sure. However, that bright and pleasing image example will help you fix in your mind the process. I now bid you good day, Miss Suzy. I look forward to our next time of sharing in this way.

FEAR

S: Matthew, do distant negative thought forms contribute to heavy emotional issues people deal with? For instance, if someone is very afraid of something, is more fear added by a matching thought form in the universe?

MATTHEW: Yes, that is exactly what happens. Any strong emotion attracts to the person a magnification of the focused object or situation. However, fear is such a powerful emotion and has so much energy within it that the object or situation feared is pulled out of the energy mainstream and magnified in accordance with the intensity of the person's feelings.

As an example, you are not attracted to risky situations such as mountain climbing or underwater sports. However, you aren't preoccupied with fearful thoughts of those activities, you simply don't engage in them. Others may actually fear those same activities but not avoid them. Conquering specific fears may be a lesson selected in their pre-birth agreements, and so they pursue risky undertakings that can engender those fears. If the fears are conquered during the activity, nothing occurs to produce a feared outcome. Climbers make the ascents and descents without incident and divers safely engage in their pursuits. But if fear enters into those activities and they can't conquer it, that energy attracts in corresponding intensity whatever is feared—an injury or even death, the ultimate in fear fulfillment.

I'll give you another example of how this works. You

have no interest in target shooting and you abhor the killing of animals for sport, so you do have occasional thoughts and feelings about guns. But those don't include fear, so your feelings about guns are only mildly registered. If you did feel strongly fearful about the very existence of guns, that would be correspondingly registered and you would attract a situation wherein a gun would present the grave danger you feared. It could be as a victim of a random drive-by shooting or a mass killing scene. That is, you don't have to intentionally participate in an event that would present the danger you feared.

Some people are intensely afraid of death from any cause. Of course they're going to die sometime, but those who are obsessed with an inordinate fear of death call forces to them that bring on their death at a much younger age than if they did not have that intense preoccupation with it.

S: Maybe that fear and early death are part of their pre-birth agreement.

MATTHEW: Maybe so. Or it may have been a lesson the individual chose for learning to overcome and failed.

ENERGY FLUCTUATION, BALANCE

MATTHEW: A combination of events and effects is challenging all humankind in this moment of Earth's history. Each person is a microcosm not only of Earth but of the universe, where immense intergalactic energy shifts are happening. Some is at levels that are counteracted and the fallout on your planet is minimal, but Earth is going through an extensive cleansing process to rid herself of the massive negativity that has been building for millennia as humans have brutalized each other and Earth's other life forms, and this is having pronounced effects on all of you. People become unbalanced because of pockets of unreleased or unusual energy, and the result of the *dis*-ease is disease. Illness, depression, mood swings and nervousness are becoming increasingly common due to the inescapable effects of the unusual energy activity.

An example of this activity is the acceleration of energy motion, which you are sensing as time passing faster and faster. Your time structure by clocks and calendars to catalog sequences of events doesn't exist outside your world, and it is coming to an end there. The reality is that everything in this universe happens in the continuum, the immeasurable vastness where all lifetimes of all souls are a series of simultaneous events. The energy frequencies are "crunching" your time measurements, and in this moment almost four days are passing in the same span that only one day used to pass. Although the acceleration has become distinctly noticeable during the past few years, it started many years prior to that.

Another effect of the time-crunch is that moon stages no longer are totally synchronized with the tides, but by divine intent, ocean movement is minimally affected to prevent disastrous results. After planetary cleansing has ended, tidal energy will return to its original calmness and the clarity of the oceans and seas once again will reflect a blue heaven.

A major source of unsettling and unexplainable sensations is the electricity generated by external sources that is interrupting the usual flow within your own electrical systems. This interference is partially caused intentionally by a manmade integrated electrical grid system that affects everyone on the planet. The grid's low frequency waves are disrupting natural electrical currents in the atmosphere and short-circuiting bodies' own electrical system. Further, it is the cumulative effect of all Earth's life forms' reactions to this situation that is affecting each person.

That infusion of disruptive current is meant to have widespread negative effects and is another example of the powerful dark, or negative, forces' influence on Earth—that is, the individuals who conceived the idea of the grid are operating under that kind of influence. Most of the people who are operating it are unaware of the dark intent behind it, which is to adversely affect your functioning by overloading your bodies' electrical systems and keep you out of balance. Because balance is so vital to your ability to absorb light and because light is essential for spiritual clarity, keeping you out of balance is a foremost aim of the dark forces.

The grid has other insidious purposes. Purportedly it is for global communications and monitoring of weather, but it is designed to manipulate weather with serious negative effects and to initiate geophysical events for the purpose of causing widespread death and destruction. It also is designed to provide surveillance of the populace worldwide and eventually control you all by that means. These dark intentions are creating negativity as well.

The dark forces are not the only source of energy direction emanating from beyond Earth's surface. Light energy also is being heavily beamed at the planet to raise your vibratory rates in preparation for the ascension of Earth and its life forms out of the current third density energy plane and into the fourth. The combination of the dark energy and the light energy has caused or exacerbated a variety of physical and emotional anomalies such as intermittent ringing of the ears, gas within body cavities, light-headedness, short-term memory loss, mood swings, anxiety, depression, uncomfortable muscular sensations and severe headaches.

Despite the aggravations caused by the opposing force fields, the infusion of light energy at this time is not only totally benevolent, it is imperative! The more light energy you absorb, the less you will be adversely affected by the efforts of the dark forces to keep you out of balance.

Here are suggestions to lessen physical and emotional discomfort and assist your system in restoring balance. Drink a lot of liquid—especially pure water, but all healthful liquids will be beneficial. There is greater need for this than ever before, as the fluids will permit the disruptive current to flow through your body more smoothly and you will not be as severely affected by it.

Relax or sleep whenever you can to keep your body in a rested, tranquil condition. Reduce tension from any source by using common sense and diligence in the knowledge that relief from stress helps counter the disquieting effects of the swirling energy. Any negative feelings will be exacerbated, so avoid unpleasant encounters as much as possible. When stressful situations must be addressed, use the spiritual approach of surrounding the person or condition with light and be in balance yourself when you start to deal with those situations.

Do not drink alcohol or use harmful drugs and do not smoke. Their components not only create stronger addiction to the substances, they interact with the grid's current to increase the harmful effects on your body's electrical system and thereby reinforce mental, physical and emotional imbalance. Consider once again the vital aspect of balance in the life of every soul and you can see how darkly effective that grid is!

If you want to quell the personal tempests during this time when multiple processes are at work to unbalance you, it is your inner voice, your "higher self," the godself wherein optimum help lies. Just ask for balance! You must maintain balance amidst the turmoil existing throughout your known world, which is only a microcosm of the ongoing intergalactic struggle for power and survival.

This is to inform you, Mother, not to frighten you! Fear and confusion come from not knowing what is happening, calmness can come from knowledge. Calmness starts with one person and extends through successive individuals coming to grips with their survival modes. Thinking beyond the confusing feelings is critical, and visualizing light surrounding Earth is a positive energy influence that I cannot emphasize too much.

It does not help those who are fearful and hurting for you to feel grave concern to the extent that it takes your own energy out of balance, out of harmonious flow. I surely do not mean that people should be without compassion or caring—balance NEVER means indifference! Indifference would only spread negativity. But it is not beneficial to you or the sufferers or the benevolent energy forces if you become so emotionally caught up in the negative aspects of happenings that you become bound by them. That is precisely what the malevolent forces are working with all their might to achieve!

S: Matthew, I feel overwhelmed. Why is life here so complex?

MATTHEW: Mother dear, life wouldn't be so complex if everyone knew that each person is a part of God and that even one person's energy is so powerful that it affects multitudes. That is why converting a negative attitude into a positive one is so important. Consider a casual conversation: The tone can be either upbeat or downtrodden, and it not only correspondingly affects those conversing, but it has far-reaching beneficial or harmful ripple effects as those people spread their sensations.

A smile is irresistible! The natural reaction to a smile results in positive energy movement that replaces the negative pockets holding psyches captive. That kind of positive attitude can do more to assist Earth to relieve her travail than any other actions at your level. Smiling is beaming goodness to all around you, and the ripple effect is incomparable in its scope of betterment. You could say it is *living* a prayer.

S: Matthew, can you explain why living among these tall fir trees means so much to me?

MATTHEW: Trees interact with your energy at a

great rate of stimulation and motion, almost drawing you into them for balancing any imbalance from conditions or circumstances. Trees always have been a source of emotional healing, and so have beloved pets. You can see evidence of this when a sick person is reunited with a beloved animal, the sparkle and uplifted spirits that the reunion imparts to both. You see this in your own life, Mother, in the joy you derive from the six dogs you've adopted. On Earth, animals and plants give far more healing energy than they draw from humans, but in this realm, the flow from the origins of the shared energy is in harmony always.

Healing is the process of leaving *dis*-ease and achieving balance, which is the perfect state of health. Some souls are blessed with either circumstances or innate ability to have balance with far less effort than others, but they have earned this bliss. Some choose to live their lifetimes without balance in even a moment, with the lifetime itself being the balance for another lifetime of predominant peacefulness.

Balance is not a given, it is worked for, earned. It is not a static condition, as flux is constant and therefore the balancing action is in continuous motion. Balance is achieved only in that instant of the absolute centering of energetic forces. It is the degrees of angles on the experiencing teeter-totter that determine whether one achieves predominantly fulfillment in a lifetime or does not. Obviously, the smaller the angle in teeter-totter motion, the more fulfillment one feels, as the center of force within maintains itself quite steadily on a course of only slight motion and the life energy force remains in finer attunement.

Balance is the greatest attainment in emotions because the most healthful flow of energy is within balance. Emotional balance is impeded by negativity, it is enhanced by loving. Extend compassion and blessings to all persons because you do not know their souls except at your own soul level. Walking among you are people whose souls have evolved far beyond the majority of us here in Nirvana as well as people whose free will choices have plunged their souls into base density. Only at soul level, not at conscious level, can you distinguish which is which.

Because each of us is a cell of the universe, we are not divorced for an instant from all that is in motion within the universe. However, we are given balancing potential that, if developed through free will choices that produce positive thought forms and positive energy, will permit that idyllic sensation for the individual even as the universe is struggling to hold its own in balancing.

True, if the universe is in turmoil, no life form can escape this struggling sensation; however, the universe is in continuous balancing activity and has the ability to keep alignment rather steady. Each of us affects the stability of the universe with every action, every feeling and every thought, however insignificant in our regard. The combination of all the thought forms produced throughout the universe IS the universe!

INTERACTION OF NEGATIVE FEELINGS

MATTHEW: Strong negative feelings about any situation can set in motion energy that will impede the course from its natural unfolding. This pertains not only to an individual's attitude, but the feelings of others who are close to him. For instance, anxiety or expectations of failure on the part of family and close associates can adversely affect the outcome of a person's situation. Their feelings would have less effect than the same feelings within that person, but negative feelings from any source do affect his situation.

Let us suppose that you express genuine good wishes to a friend about a job interview, but you are doubtful about a successful outcome. Your doubt sends forth energy without malice, but with deterrent effects nonetheless. The negative thought forms of your doubt add their own independent effects to the universal soup with specific influence directed toward your friend, and that energy swirls around her situation. And if the friend has any self-doubt, her feelings will home in on the "doubting" negativity in thought forms from every other source and by the laws of the universe, her self-doubt will be amplified.

Thought forms cannot distinguish between "good" anxiety and "bad" anxiety, only the strength of the emotion. Motive and intent are indeed registered, but they are apart from the emotion itself, which is registered only in intensity. That intensity is why prayer works. It's why voodoo works, too.

PART III

OUR SOUL CONNECTION

THE SOUL

S: I know the soul is our eternal connection with God and Creator, but I don't know exactly what the soul is or what it does.

MATTHEW: The soul is the very essence of life as it first sprang from Creator. It is an indestructible living entity of light energy that may have a physical body, etheric body or astral body, or it may exist in free spirit only. Our souls, manifested by God through His co-creating powers with Creator, are expressions of the love and light of God and contain in microcosm every essence of God. In any of its forms, the soul is an inviolate independent being at the same time it exists inseparably with God and Creator and all other souls in the cosmos.

The body is only a very fleeting vehicle for use by the soul, which is *far* stronger and more tenacious than any third density body such as those of Earth humankind. And, the body does not hold the soul, the soul creates the body from its image that will fit the specific experiencing it chooses in each incarnate lifetime. When the soul is released from the physical body, its etheric body is released at that same instant, and in that etheric body the soul makes its lightning-fast transition from Earth to Nirvana, the change from a physical life to a life in spirit that you call "death."

The soul is the power behind everything that exists on Earth. It is the life force of all its parts that it creates for ever-greater experiencing. At every level of evolvement, each soul part is an independent self with intelligence,

characteristics, choices, goals and all the other life
elements that make each person a unique being.

Each individual lifetime of a soul is its personage. The
sum of a soul's personages is the cumulative soul, in which
all knowledge gained by each personage is available to all.
Thus, as each melds into the cumulative soul, bringing
the wisdom of that lifetime's experiences, every individual
personage evolves just as the cumulative soul does.

Mother, I know the question in your mind. It's an
important point, so before I continue, please write it for
the record.

*S: Thank you, dear. Where does ego fit into the
individual soul that you call the personage?*

MATTHEW: Ego is the part of the personage that is
self-identity and self-worth in accordance with efforts and
accomplishments. But just as honoring those is not the
same as vanity, honoring ego as a reflection of one's self-
identity is not the same as being egotistical. The sense of
self is essential to the personage, yet often "ego" in that
context is overshadowed by its derivations "egotistical,"
"egocentric" and "egotism" that define an individual who
is focused solely on self, who relates everything about
others to his own needs or desires and has a "puffed-up"
impression of his characteristics and achievements. That
kind of person is considered pompous and conceited,
without a shred of humility, and unpleasant to be around.

However, much more serious than having an
unpleasing personality is that without any sense of the
humility that is a natural and automatic aspect of
spiritual growth, that person is stagnating in soul
evolution. Spiritual growth is the molding of one's ego in
ways that are aligned with the soul contract.

Remember, this is a time for ending third density experiencing, a time when soul contract choices are designed to overcome traits that are counterproductive to spiritual growth and to enhance qualities that foster that growth.

S: *How can we know if we're "honoring" our accomplishments or being vain about them?*

MATTHEW: You know by the fulfilling feelings like self-confidence that you are making your best effort in whatever you are undertaking and the self-respect that comes with that sensation; self-determination to live in godly ways; self-assurance that you are being or becoming the "who" your soul signed up to be; self-awareness that you are a part of God and inseparable from the Oneness of Creation.

S: *But what if the ego "tells" people they're right in what they believe about themselves, but actually they are being negatively influenced by the darkness?*

MATTHEW: Attaching itself to the ego is precisely how the darkness operates, and the ramifications go far beyond *"Is it vanity or humility?"* The darkness shrouds self-identity with the delusion that the person's convictions are absolutely correct about what is true and what is false, and it firmly resists thoughts that threaten those assertions or could lessen the ego's stubbornness in holding fast to them. This produces the closed mind, or, in your common expression, "the box." Just as it applies to all other forms of dark influence, love is the key to opening that boxed-up mind and letting the light come in.

S: Thank you, dear. One more thing—am I right in thinking that the soul's consciousness is infinitely greater than the ego's consciousness?

MATTHEW: You are indeed, Mother, and just how "infinitely" greater is what I intended to explain before I interrupted myself to reply to your mental questioning. The consciousness of the soul has the capability to reach all knowledge and wisdom that exists throughout creation. The universal mind—the entire spectrum of human and godly powers and all experiencing throughout this universe's existence—is within each soul. When the soul taps into this knowing, it reports what it "sees" to the brain, which is a personal computer that processes data for the mind to assimilate and contemplate. The key to achieving this is to quiet your thoughts so you can "hear" the messages from your soul that may come as images or words or impressions or a combination.

S: Matthew, I can't even imagine what all is in the universal mind!

MATTHEW: Mother dear, no third density brain has that kind of comprehension. It is at soul level that this kind of communication occurs. It is your soul experiencing this lifetime that is tapping into the fullness of information within your cumulative soul.

THE CUMULATIVE SOUL

S: Matthew, I'm confused about what the cumulative soul is.

MATTHEW: All of this is new to you, Mother, and it's understandable that it is difficult to grasp. I believe this is the simplest explanation of the cumulative soul: It is the composite of all its parts starting with the very first division of itself into an independent lifetime for diversity in experiencing.

S: OK, thank you, dear! Where do cumulative souls reside?

MATTHEW: There is no specific place of residence because a cumulative soul is not an individual entity, but rather the indivisible sum of all its personages wherever they are living, and it grows as each one adds its lifetime experiences to the ever-changing composite. Actually, a better description of a cumulative soul than I first gave you is that it is a force field that derives its entire essence from all its aspects wherever they are throughout the universe.

S. That does make it easier to understand—thank you. Do you personally know the other personages in your cumulative soul or do you only have access to their knowledge?

MATTHEW: I know those who are in this realm and

some of us have become friends. Some are spending a
lifetime on Earth, and I know very well who they are!
Some have progressed so far toward the light of God that
our densities are incompatible, so a meeting isn't possible,
and others have regressed far from the light into lower
densities, and I'm surely not interested in going there!
Some have chosen lifetimes out of this galaxy, where I
don't travel often, so I'm barely acquainted with them.

Each has its own soul growth to accomplish, Mother.
Wherever the other personages are living for their
individual growth, we're always within the familial
bonding of our cumulative soul. But it isn't necessary
that we meet or share interests or know all the details of
each other's lives. What we do share is the essential
knowledge of our collective experiencing, otherwise all
the individual souls' learning would be wasted. And, not
to add a complexity here but rather to explain how the
cumulative soul has such comprehensive knowledge: All
the personages are living simultaneously in the timeless
continuum, so not only "past" but also "future" lifetimes
are feeding into that force field—it's not only "old"
knowledge that is there for each personage to tap into.

The cumulative soul can advance from its station
toward the light only by the advancement of its personages.
Therefore, each personage not only has the benefit of the
cumulative soul's composite knowledge, but it is continuously given encouragement at soul level to master its
chosen lessons so the cumulative soul can evolve.
However, that is not self-serving—with that soul's
advancement, all of its personages also have the
opportunity to evolve. But, depending upon its use of
free will choices, each of the personages can either grow
toward the light or regress so far as to become trapped
in base energy.

S: *If a personage becomes trapped, how does that affect its cumulative soul's energy?*

MATTHEW: The lifetime energy registration that consigns a personage to the base energy placement does not affect its cumulative soul because that personage's unique energy stream made its own way entirely by its free will choices. The cumulative soul may encourage its personages, but it can't ever interfere with their free will. However, out of love for all its personages, the cumulative soul may request divine grace to assist any that become trapped in base energy.

S: *Are the individual souls always aware of everything their cumulative soul knows?*

MATTHEW: Let me compare this with your memory, Mother. Nothing you have learned or experienced is ever lost in your memory system, but you can't remember everything at the same time—it would be overwhelming! Furthermore, many of your experiences were so trivial that they were irrelevant to subsequent happenings and never returned to your conscious mind, yet all are in your memory bank. It's the same with the personages of the cumulative soul as they experience their respective lifetimes.

S: *That makes sense. Matthew, with all these parts of your cumulative soul, I just want to be absolutely sure that you are ONLY my Matthew and nobody else!*

MATTHEW: Oh, Mother, absolutely I am Matthew and no one else! Every personage is its own soul and no one else! The cumulative soul is the synthesis of all its soul-selves that are completely independent beings.

S: *But it sounds as if every soul that divides itself becomes a cumulative soul, so you could do the same and become one, too.*

MATTHEW: Mother, I realize that in my eagerness to answer your questions, sometimes my efforts result in confusion rather than clarification. The terms I've given you for the various aspects of soul expression—cumulative soul, personages, soul fragments or sparks and such— are meant only to show the soul's long journey striving through multiple lifetimes to return to its Beginnings in the perfect love and light of Creator.

In this realm we don't need differentiation of terms because each soul's energy registration in the universe is evidence of its evolutionary station. Since each soul is its own inviolate self regardless of its station or the number of its progeny, we think of each simply as "soul." And that is how we speak of each one to you unless we are trying to explain the soul growth stages through its independently functioning aspects, or the inextricable and eternal connection of each soul with God and all other souls in the universe.

A most relevant point here is what I mentioned about all souls' lifetimes within the continuum, where there is no linear time basis for the dividing and subdividing into independently experiencing entities. The simultaneous "past" "present" and "future" lives of the cumulative soul are simply in different life forms in different stages of development in different placements in the universe. However, you can't comprehend the timelessness of the continuum or imagine living simultaneously in many different kinds of bodies in many different worlds because you aren't consciously aware of those lifetimes. Therefore, we can only try to explain by using your linear time, calling the various lifetimes "reincarnation," and placing it all within a spiritual hierarchical structure that can fit into your understanding.

I still may not have clarified this enough, Mother, but the good news is that you will understand this seemingly unfathomable mystery when your soul has returned to Nirvana.

S: I'll count on that for later, but I'd like to know NOW if you and I have the same cumulative soul.

MATTHEW: We certainly do, Mother! I was hoping you would ask, but if you hadn't, I would have told you. You and I have such similar energy levels, or vibrations, and special bonding because we go back almost to our cumulative soul's "birth" in antiquity in a universal placement far beyond Earth; and our lives on the planet began probably half a million or so years ago in your counting of time, maybe even lots farther back than that. Some of our family and dearest other people later came into what became our "soul cluster," but others were introduced down the line from other cumulative souls when we needed them or vice versa.

∽ ✿✿✿ ∾

ENTRY OF DARKNESS

*S: I've heard the term "root soul"—is that another
name for the cumulative soul?*

MATTHEW: No. The root soul began in deepest
antiquity, after the gift of free will and its power of
manifestation was bestowed by Creator upon Its original
soul creations—the archangels, who were pure spirit.
Eons later, acting upon their idea to make souls with
potential for experiencing in a physical form, they and
Creator co-created those kinds of souls. By making those
"new" souls, the co-creators became the first "cumulative"
souls and the beings they produced are the "root souls."

*S: I think I understand now what they are. Or is
there something else I need to know about them?*

MATTHEW: Oh yes, Mother, a great deal more! You
could say that we took some important detours and now
are back on the main highway.

Although the soul is indestructible, its light energy
can be captured by negativity and trapped within density
so powerful that eventually the soul descends into
Nirvana's basest, or densest, energy layer. By the most
ancient universal law, at physical death the lifetime
energy generated by the transitioning soul automatically
takes it to the placement it needs for healing and learning.
The people who repeatedly chose to use their free will in
ungodly ways during multiple physical lifetimes, thus
creating their own deeper and deeper density, eventually

are drawn by that natural law to the densest energy part of this multilayered spirit realm.

Those are people who again and again chose to control others' lives or inflict brutality or be tyrannical rulers, or who are so steeped in rage, greed, prejudice, deceit or other intense negativity that every aspect of their lives is permeated with thoughts, feelings and actions born of those kinds of negativity. Through hundreds or perhaps thousands of such lifetimes, those souls continued spiraling downward from the light until finally they reached Nirvana's basest density. Not only is escape beyond their brain capacity at that primitive stage of mental comprehension, but the energy of that placement, which is aligned with their own, holds them captive.

S: Does that mean that souls of people like Hitler can't reincarnate to cause more atrocities because they can't get out of that placement?

MATTHEW: They can leave only if they move toward the light that is continuously beamed to them from highest light sources. If they do respond to the love vibrations within that light, they will be entirely different souls as they rise to successively higher layers of the realm.

But even if that happens, it is not the full story. Their very descent to the basest energy placement has inestimable negative repercussions. The energy set in motion by their Earth lifetimes remains when their physical bodies leave, and the influence left by their energy is not diminished. The ripple effect of the devastation wrought by just one such individual can be so injurious to civilization that there is no way to assess it separately from the base energies that form from it. So, while the energy of that individual soul is held captive, the energy of the negative effects of its lifetime remains, and the dark forces gather it unto themselves for rearmament, so to speak.

S: You told me that Nirvana is made up of differing density layers, but I can't imagine where this base layer could be. Actually, I can't understand why it's even a part of your world, Matthew!

MATTHEW: Mother, I know this is not your Presbyterian division of heaven and hell, but where would you have those souls go if not here? This is the only place Earth residents can go after physical death, and Nirvana's composition is designed to accommodate every one of them—all the people deemed "godly" or "saved" and all the people deemed "evil."

Let me back up for a moment so you can get a clearer picture. Remember my telling you that this realm's many flexible, independent but interconnected energy layers are near your moon? The lowest layer is the one closest to the moon, where it is surrounded by a density that isn't correctly known to your scientists. After the moon was cut off from its original planetary structure and became devoid of natural conditions that would sustain what you would call "real" life, it became a dumping ground for universally-rejected matter. The non-inhabitability of that area makes it a good place for housing the base energy souls.

There is still another part of this spirit world and it is separate from the rest—that is the home of souls with the basest energy. They are confined within a tiny orbiting sphere that cannot be seen by your scientists even though it is only about a hundred miles from Earth.

S: That's so close to us, Matthew!

MATTHEW: It's natural that you would think in terms of miles, Mother, but distance isn't relevant. Due to its density, that tiny orb cannot be pulled in by the planet's gravitational field, so it never will touch the planet; and the souls' energy density, which is the same as the orb's, won't let them escape from it. However, that density does have an effect on Earth's peoples because it permits the release of sparks, like sparks from an overloaded electrical wire, that are attracted to souls whose energy is even somewhat compatible with base energy.

I have spoken about the Earth "puppets" of the off-planet dark forces that wish to control the planet—the connection between the puppets and their puppet masters is those sparks. They are not light, but rather a frequency of very low vibration that acts something like a decorative net sweeping the ocean floor to attract, then entrap, curious sea life. Humans who are curious about the sensations that come with indulging in heinous activities are drawn into and trapped in a "net" of low vibrations. Satanic worship with its unconscionable tortures and sacrifices of human and animal life is a prime example of the basest density energy in action.

S: Is that the energy that started with Lucifer? Or is Lucifer only a name that religion gave a "fallen angel" and it's actually just energy being directed into evil ways?

MATTHEW: As for the name Lucifer, or any name given to the archangels and other high light beings, they are indeed proper names of the various entity forces that your science recognizes only as forms of energy. Each entity is its own power, some with such vastness that it cannot even be imagined on Earth, so it is understandable that science doesn't personalize these powers with names. But consider this: Why would the myriad souls co-created by God and Creator not have names to distinguish their individual, inviolate selves from all others, just as all relatives in any family do?

Now then, Lucifer was created in Creator's first expression of individual parts, that highest realm of angels whom you call archangels. Once free will was bestowed upon those souls, they could choose what to co-create in subsequent manifestations. Originally Lucifer had good intent to create equally with Creator, who had only light to impart to Its creations. But eventually Lucifer delighted in using his free will and curiosity to make terrible and miserable creatures, and that dropped him into increasingly baser density. As the Luciferian energy core grew with each intentional horrible manifestation, it divided again and again; and with each division, the souls with that energy voluntarily withdrew farther and farther from Creator, away from the light of their Source into the density of darkness.

What exists on Earth today is a continuation of that withdrawal from the light, and individuals who are carrying out the bidding of the dark forces are operating in that dense Luciferian energy. Energy is neutral, remember, and "Luciferian energy" is only a term for the energy that in deepest antiquity, Lucifer kept directing toward baser and still baser activities.

S: Are Lucifer's soul descendants born with his darkness and can't get themselves out of it?

MATTHEW: Lucifer was created of total light, so the first of his lineage could only be of light. But there is light within every incarnated soul regardless of its ancestry, just as there is free will to follow the light or not. As Lucifer fell from the light due to his free will choices, his progeny were not automatically drawn down with him. Those who used their own free will to join him on his downward spiral were continuously "beamed" light all along the way—some chose to return to the light, some did not. Those who did not are spoken of as the dark forces, as the energy of their thought forms became part of that vast force field of negativity.

S: I see. Where in the universe do the dark forces reside?

MATTHEW: Wherever they wish within dimensions of density where the vibratory level cannot trap their psyches. The most powerful of the dark energies usually do not embody, although they have the manifesting capability to make bodies of any design and whatever else they want to create *EXCEPT souls and light*. That is why the light forces ultimately will overcome the dark forces—the dark energies never can spread their darkness enough to snuff out the last vestiges of light!

ALWAYS the most powerful is Creator! If Creator wishes to extinguish the life force of souls at the peak of the darkness, this can be done. At any moment Creator so decides, those souls can be reabsorbed and neutralized.

LOST SOULS

S: What do you mean, a soul can be "reabsorbed and neutralized"?

MATTHEW: Mother, I feel your great confusion, so even though I have spoken about many facets of souls, I'll start at the beginning and pull it all together. The Christed light realm is Creator's first expression of Itself and where the pure essence of love-light is infinite and eternal. From those Beginnings, individual souls, or personages throughout the cosmos, at every level from the angelic realm souls to their most recent "offspring," have free will with *proportionally* the same properties of Creator, and in this universe, of God.

Every one of the personages is inseparable from its parent soul, yet is an independent being with its own personality, options, ideas, goals and all other elements that make an individual unique. This uniqueness never is lost or diminished even though that individual soul is a part of a larger, then still larger, then even larger soul grouping that includes ALL the personages of that same original soul—the root soul—that was created in deepest antiquity. Regardless of how many personages may be in its lineage throughout countless ages, the root soul *always* remains its independent, inviolate self with free will. So does every one of its personages, and the experiencing of the root soul has no hold whatsoever on their free will choices.

If the root soul chooses a path of violence and brutality, it drops from the light and falls into a density compatible with its actions and temperament, where its free will choices become narrowed and weighted by density. As the soul's psyche, which is what determines attitudes and intentions, becomes more and more prone to what you call evil and its deeds become more and more horrible, its free will is correspondingly lessened in ability to recognize the light, and its conscience atrophies from lack of use. Your word "unconscionable" derives from that loss of a functioning conscience.

Meanwhile, all of that root soul's personages are exercising their own free will wherever they are living in the continuum. Some may choose a lifetime of violence, corruption, greed or other kind of base energy attachment, while others choose to live within the light. Regardless of the choices and consequences of the individual personages, the root soul's pathway away from the light is recorded *only* in its lifeprint in the Akashic Records and the experiencing of all its personages is recorded only in their individual lifeprints in the records.

Ideally, free will choices lead to spiritual clarity, which is one's conscious awareness of inseparability with God. This is the pathway to reintegration with God and Creator, and as such, it is the element of all lives that is so vitally in need of development! Or, more accurately, of *conscious remembrance*, because this clarity does exist in the cellular memory of each soul. However, a soul that uses its free will for negative choices piles one layer of forgetfulness upon another and it recedes farther and farther from spiritual clarity.

Without that clarity, a soul's choices for dark, exploitative experimentation and activities become ingrained in its psyche's desire channels, and the soul becomes a slave of those desires. The multiple lifetimes of a root soul's personages can span millions of your

calendar years while the root soul itself spirals downward until finally it is so mired in darkness that it is
captive of its own energy in Nirvana's most intense
density level, that tiny orbiting sphere. To keep the soul
from sliding into total darkness, light forces give it
special attention to reinforce its only remaining light,
the spark that is its life force. Despite their awareness
that the soul's course is closing in on "lost soul" status,
the light forces must honor its free will to pursue its
direction toward that destiny.

For the souls that descend to that depth, Creator
provides an angel of the highest power and brilliance of
light to be the over-angel. In the balance essential for
achieving soul growth, there must be balance in this
sense as well. The lost souls are in the most desperate
need of balance, and only from the highest angelic realm
can there be a counterforce equal to the task.

In this connection there is constant light visible at a
pinpoint, with love beamed steadily and intensely into
the region of the lost souls. Every soul there has the
opportunity to draw closer and closer to that light, and as
many souls as wish to progress toward it can do so simultaneously. Only once within the light has redemption
been accomplished. Creator's love-light essence is infinite
and eternal, therefore the Christed love-light is also.

Some of the lost souls do respond to the extraordinary
efforts on behalf of their redemption, and there is great
rejoicing at these triumphant outcomes. The souls who
persistently refuse the light are captured by the dark
forces that successfully waged battle with them throughout
all their lifetimes, eventually draining them of all
memory and light. At the end of those eons of combat,
the captives of the dark forces are useless to them because
they have become no more than totally unmotivated,

pathetic creatures without even a memory of a spark of Christed light. Thus, not only useless but no longer even a challenge, they are abandoned by the dark forces, whose victory is that where once there was light, now there is none except the connective spark to Creator.

The abandoned beings are lost souls. Only Creator can deem a soul to be lost and decree reabsorption—only Creator is powerful enough to reabsorb and neutralize that intensely base energy. In actuality, a soul that has been reabsorbed is not truly "lost" because it is within the core essence of Creator, but never again will it have a single focused mind nor will it be able to fragment into personages with free will and vitality.

But the most profound and tragic impact when this happens to a root soul is that all of its personages are inextricably related to its destiny, and what *is* irretrievably lost is that soul's ability to continue providing life force to its lineage. The soul is the source of any being's life force, and the root soul is the source of the life force of all of its personages throughout all existence. When the root soul is reabsorbed into Creator, at that moment it no longer has life force to provide to them—their physical bodies die and the souls themselves also are reabsorbed into Creator's essence. That is why there is such great sadness when the few root souls who persisted to that fate did so—they extinguished the life force of all their progeny too.

I hasten to say that the personages are lost only at soul level, not at memory level. Their lifetimes cannot be expunged from their own records or the records of all the individuals in whose lives they participated.

S: Do you mean that those souls still exist by being in the memory of souls who are alive?

MATTHEW: No, memory is separate from body and soul life forces. Memory has its own energy field and that is what lives on. Those souls do remain in the memories of anyone whose life they deeply touched, but those memories are a province only of the remembering persons and have nothing whatsoever to do with the reabsorbed souls' memory energy.

S: I see. What happens to positive karma the personages accrued?

MATTHEW: It is transmuted into energy that serves to balance the lives adversely affected by the death of any personage of the root soul that had no opportunity to achieve karmic balancing. Often karma is played out with the same individuals participating—that is, within a soul cluster—but it's not required, so that positive karma can be applied in the same measure via a different means. It could be a lesson in agreement with others or perhaps by a universal righting of an imbalance due to the reabsorption of the root soul. However the karmic energy is applied, it is an example of divine grace at work.

S: How would the death of a root soul affect its personages in Nirvana?

MATTHEW: Here or in any other discarnate realm, those lives are affected the same as the souls in physical form. The level of evolvement they have attained in their multiple physical and spirit lifetimes and their current experiencing in any civilization in this universe are not factors in this. When the soul life force is cut at the root, it is the same as if a main electrical power source is cut— it no longer can supply energy to any of its auxiliary stations, so all of those are powerless too. When the root soul's life force is gone, so is the life force of all souls in its lineage.

S: But when those who are on Earth die, if they can't go to Nirvana, where do they go? Where's their "eternal life"?

MATTHEW: When the life force of the root soul is discontinued, there's simply no life force left to take any of its personages anywhere. Because their energy force field can't be abolished or destroyed, it is returned to Creator, the source of all energy in the cosmos. The individual lifetime memories of those souls remain in energy form, as I mentioned, and energy definitely is eternal, Mother!

S: Yes, I see, but still.... So, how can we know if our root soul is close to lost soul status?

MATTHEW: Neither at conscious level nor at soul level can this be known, nor should it be. There is absolutely nothing that can be done to change any soul's status within the lineage and nothing any soul can do about their root soul's fate. But there is a soul preservation mechanism that shields this impending fate of the lineage souls in this universe. The Christed light envelops them in most tender vibrations for the transit into the realm of God where they live in memory energy status. At that station they are almost in a slumbering state from which they could awaken if the dispensation process is approved.

Dispensation petitions have been offered on behalf of the lost and nearly lost souls to permit a soul level cleansing, an

awakened spiritual clarity as to the depths of density into
which they have fallen, where only primitive instinct
exists. Dispensation would be the highest council of the
universe granting these souls permission to quickly rise
into a density with intelligence and reasoning ability,
thus offering them a greatly accelerated opportunity to
make more enlightened choices than previously. If this
occurs, all lineage of the lost root souls would be included,
and angels and soulmates have volunteered to assist in
this soul-saving operation.

S: *Why hasn't this been done before now?*

MATTHEW: This planetary cleansing era at hand is
unlike any others that have preceded it. Its effects are
meant to liberate not only Earth's peoples, but souls
anywhere in the universe whose lives are being
controlled by the dark forces that act like puppet
masters manipulating the strings of their puppets. It is
the same petition for soul cleansing at that universal
level as on Earth and in this realm, but on a far grander
scale than our microcosmic struggle for survival.

S: *Thank you for explaining all of this, Mash dear.*

MATTHEW: Mother, dearest soul to me, you are
welcome!

2008:

*S: Matthew, you gave me that information in 1994—
has the petition been granted since then?*

MATTHEW: Not exactly, Mother—that is, not as it
was conceived, but there is a joyous development that is
even more profound! What we know at this station,
which is considerably more advanced than the general
populations of Nirvana and Earth, is that Earth's
ascension is part of universal changes that offer the soul
cleansing aspect of redemption throughout this universe.
As such, it is embracing in ever-increasing light intensity
the souls in all physical and spirit worlds who are
foundering, and those who choose to respond positively
will continue life in their respective placements. Now, if
among those souls who respond positively are personages
of a root soul that has nearly reached reabsorption, they
will NOT lose their life force if reabsorption occurs; by
divine grace, in that same instant they will be infused
with light from other sources and without a blink, their
lives will go on.

Also, the progeny of all lost souls will "reawaken" and
be reconnected with their memory energy. After a period
of adjustment, which will include "updating" of all
happenings during their slumbering state within God,
they will examine their lifeprints and choose the next
appropriate level of experiencing in physical form. The
collective energy of the reabsorbed root souls will be
released into the universe as diffused light.

*S. That IS a joyous development! What is diffused
light and how does it differ from "ordinary" light?*

MATTHEW: As celestial bodies die from implosion or explosion in a collision, their parts go whirling through space until they reach a gravitational field that pulls them into its mass, and along the way friction erodes miniscule dots of living matter—those dots are diffused light.

To explain its difference from "ordinary" light, I'll give you an analogy, Mother. Light is a powerful energy force that can be directed instantly by thoughts, like clay can be used immediately by a potter who knows exactly what he wants to produce. Diffused light is energy that is floating freely and is available for any potential use, like clay awaiting some form—until the potter's thoughts gel into the specific shape, size and purpose of the object he wants to make, the clay simply is there, ready for his use.

S: I see. Is there much diffused light in the universe?

MATTHEW: Good question, Mother! In the Beginnings, ALL was diffused light as Creator expressed the creating material—*energy*—from which all potential thought forms and their manifestations could be produced. Throughout the incalculable eons since then, a great deal of the diffused light has been used to co-create all that exists in this universe, with all the creating material coming from Creator and the "products" from the thought forms of countless souls.

SOUL TRANSFERENCE

S: Why can some people recover completely after being clinically dead for periods exceeding the time of usual brain death? I met a woman who had regained consciousness over 40 minutes after being pronounced dead. She had complete cognitive ability and total memory of all that had happened around her during that time lapse and her nearly lifelong crippling was healed.

MATTHEW: Mother, there are two issues here. Let's deal first with those people who fully recover after "clinical death." Say ten minutes pass in that state, which normally would cause brain damage. When that doesn't happen, it is because the love energy bonding between that person and souls here furnishes the body with a life force, but since it is below the instrument ratings of vital life signs, the person is considered dead. However, the body's minimal life force runs parallel to the far stronger love energy force that is "lifting" the soul so it can function at that stronger level, and when that same powerful energy is infused into the body, no damage results from the lapse in regular physical functioning.

This intervention would not happen if either physical death at that time or impaired functioning for the duration of the Earth lifetime is a provision of the pre-birth agreement. For the greater numbers of people who do not regain consciousness, the end of the physical lifetime usually is in accordance with their agreement provisions.

Now then, in the case of the woman who was

clinically dead for forty-some minutes, that was *soul transference*. She is known here as one of the sterling successes of that process. Hers was not a singular experience, but much more often this process occurs in people who are unconscious much longer than she, people in a comatose state, but even then it is not a commonplace occurrence.

S: What about the souls of comatose people who live in that state for weeks or months?

MATTHEW: Most often the souls of the people who recover have remained with them throughout the period of unconsciousness. Or there can be the soul transference I mentioned, and if so, that is what rejuvenates the body.

S: Please explain soul transference.

MATTHEW: When the soul of the comatose patient wishes to pursue other lessons and there is an agreement with a soul in spirit who also sees opportunities for karmic fulfillment, then preparations are made for the soul transference to the benefit of both souls. This can happen at the onset of the comatose condition or at any time as long as the body has viability. The initial signal may be made by the soul in that body or by one interested in entering a comatose body. A central registry for recording such signals alerts interested souls to the availability of a transference requester or provider.

There is another vital point here. The body must be willing to endure whatever its functioning limitations and attendant problems may be after rejuvenation, so the body's agreement to experience all the physical, mental and emotional ramifications must be considered by the two pertinent souls. No approval from other sources is required, so if the two souls and the body agree, the process is initiated.

The transference of knowledge from one soul to another is a simple process. The human brain is a computer, and just as your computer may easily be keyed to download data into a second computer or storage facility, so can the complete knowledge of the comatose soul be downloaded, or transferred, to the acquiring soul. Having left the original soul, that knowledge becomes the property of the soul entering the body. All experiencing of both souls prior to the transference was recorded instant by instant in their lifeprints in the Akashic Records, and from that point on, the same will be true—there will be no mix-up in the two souls' records.

About the physical rejuvenation aspect, the entering soul has the ability to infuse the comatose body with life force that the previous soul no longer could manage due to the extent of debilitation. Souls do not regenerate cells automatically. That life force is physical, and although a soul's will can be strong indeed, certain physiological forces are at work.

The DNA of some civilizations does not include illness, aging or death, and long ago in Earth's history, people lived far longer than today, hundreds even thousands of years, and were healthy in body, mind and spirit. That programming was manipulated by dark energies so that Earth bodies and minds became progressively frail and aged rapidly, comparatively speaking. The brain is so constrained in this indoctrination that it added a layer of aging-death belief to the cellular memory, consequently current physical constitution is feeble and so is brain power.

This has a bearing on how effectively the body can

recover, but more so, how well the brain can assimilate the downloaded knowledge. All memories, acquired knowledge and behavioral patterns are intact at soul transference, but they cannot be as well grounded as if the body and brain were in top condition at that time. Transference usually takes place after severe brain deterioration from injury or debilitating illness, and although the infusion of energy does rejuvenate the brain cells, there is slippage of details due to the body's impaired brain functioning. Thus some information is lost that the recovering person, now with the new soul, previously knew. That slippage, combined with the new soul's intent to pursue its own choices of experiencing, would certainly account for a "personality change." Even with the easily accepted explanation of memory loss due to the effects of injury or illness on the brain, the difference in personality often is shocking for the person's family and friends.

S: But with the downloaded knowledge from the original soul to the new one, why would there be such a personality difference? Aren't all of the experiences that help to form a personality still present in that knowledge?

MATTHEW: The entering soul has its own personage to take into the body. Personage is the personality of a *soul*, which is not the same as the personality of an individual. An individual's personality consists of attitudes developed during the lifetime whereas the personage is the *essence* of an individual. It is what the soul imparts: sense of honor, conscience, radiant goodness, conscious awareness of the light within, inseparable interconnectedness with God and all other souls. Depending upon the degrees of light within the original soul and the entering soul, the individual's personality may differ in quite noticeable ways that may be an enhancement or a disadvantage to existing relationships.

S: I can see that—thank you for explaining soul transference. What happens when someone's brain is so badly damaged that restoring mental functioning is impossible, but the body keeps on living?

MATTHEW: The soul may choose from several alternatives. It may remain in a state of rest within the body until physical death. It may leave and embody in a fetus that has no soul designee. It may come directly to this realm and choose from all the options here.

When a soul chooses to leave the body, physical functioning is purely by the will of the body life force, which is apart from the soul life force. This does happen in persons who may experience long-term unconsciousness, even when breathing is by the body's own ability. If the soul has chosen to leave, the bodies of persons in a mechanically-maintained living state would die if removed from that apparatus.

There is no standard time for a soul to decide in this issue. This is as personal as the decision about what to do. If the soul is experiencing a chosen lesson, the outcome is known, but when the comatose condition is not by pre-birth agreement, continuance of physical life is reevaluated. This is allowed in all cases where further experiencing would be far different from the agreement. Here again it is by divine grace that such a choice is made possible when difficult circumstances that are not part of the pre-birth agreement are introduced into the life experience.

S: OK, thank you, but what is the advantage of soul

transference over a soul entering a newborn except accelerated aging that could offer certain experiencing that waiting until later might not?

MATTHEW: Mother, that is *enough!* That *is* the purpose, and especially in this time when everything is being accelerated, the ramifications are far more extensive and advantageous than you are considering. Also, there is learning for both souls in the transference itself, and the willingness of the acquiring soul to engage in the process is vital growth—in most cases, he's not scheduled for "easy street."

2008:

S: *Matthew, are any of the souls who enter comatose bodies the "walk-ins" who came from advanced civilizations in the universe specifically to assist us during this transition to Earth's Golden Age?*

MATTHEW: If so, I don't know of them, Mother. Those bodies and especially the brains rarely offer the optimum conditions that "walk-in" souls require to function in accordance with their intentions for coming at this time. All whom I know about came some years ago either by birth into the genetic and environmental circumstances they needed to become highly influential, or their agreements for soul transference called for a hasty exit of the original soul and entry of the "walk-in" soul. In the latter case, the walk-ins choose souls with capabilities and circumstances they will need to successfully accomplish their purposes.

S: *Do you know if all of them are succeeding in what*

they came to do?

MATTHEW: I don't know how many are achieving their full potential, but I do know those who are living in alignment with their pre-birth or pre-walk-in intentions, which in all cases is to assist in bringing peace and harmony to your world. Perhaps the best known is Barack Obama, who will be elected president of the United States, but many others also have come with multiple lifetimes of leadership experience or other types of expertise to contribute to the massive changes underway that are leading to world reformation.

S: How can you tell the difference between Earth's own lightworkers and those who are from other civilizations?

MATTHEW: The DNA of souls from advanced civilizations has different patterning from souls who have attained only third density soul evolvement, and this is evident in their distinctive auras and vibrations. But Mother, many of the souls you call "Earth's own lightworkers" have had lifetimes in the advanced civilizations that lived on the planet and they are well equipped to participate in the master plan for the Golden Age —that is why they were so eager to embody there again! Among the young adults and children who came from spiritually and intellectually evolved civilizations on Earth or elsewhere in the universe are the Indigo and Crystal children, who will be the next generation's fine leaders.

PARALLEL LIVES, "PROBABLE LIVES"

S: When we say something happened "in a previous life," we mean it was a long time ago or with another mate. I thought "parallel life" was just a facetious expression too, but someone told me those lives really exist. What do you think, Matthew?

MATTHEW: Mother, it's not what I think, it's what I know! Parallel lives do indeed exist. They are types of experiencing beyond, in addition to, and separate from an individual's conscious lifetime. The parallel beings are in different points of the universe and in different eras of what you call past or future. This is how soul clusters can share so many lifetimes.

S: Oh! Well, how do those lives get started?

MATTHEW: A parallel life may be given existence at a pathway fork and it becomes the "path" not consciously traveled. The energy invested in those paths not chosen must be allowed its continuance somehow. Rarely is a person aware of the accumulated energy that is invested in non-chosen paths, so that energy must seek its own way. Energy cannot be destroyed, as you know, but neither can it be abandoned to simply exist in suspension, and it is not transmuted into the chosen path because the person doesn't know that the energy could be diverted.

Without the individual who initiated the parallel life giving its energy any direction, it pursues a course that is the logical continuance and conclusion for its beginning. Part of the continuance is derived from the natural course of the initiating momentum and part is derived from the energy of the person's subsequent thoughts, such as speculation on "What if' I had taken that other job or married that other person or gone to that other school or moved to that other city—any of the possibilities the person strongly considered at the time of choosing which pathway to take at an important fork in the road.

Parallel lives, which may be experienced in spirit or in bodies that are less dense in form than your third density bodies, do not influence the *conscious* life of the soul that originated them. There is no specially designated placement for parallel experiencing, but wherever it takes place can be termed "inner planes." Every event, circumstance and result of parallel lives is confined to the parallel placements of those entities and their independent choices. Those lives and their placements are an inseparable match, existing in union and in their own context.

S: How are those lives recorded in the Akashic Records?

MATTHEW: They aren't. There is a similar recording means for parallel lives, but that system is its own entity and is not cross-referenced with the Akashic records. This parallel recording system could be considered an autonomous division of the records, though, because the information can be available for examination by the same rules and methods applied to the Akashic records. However, the parallel files are distinctly separate from the originator's lifeprint and cannot be intermingled as part of the self-judging process at lifetime review.

S: I've been meaning to ask you where the "regular" soul's lifeprint is reviewed.

MATTHEW: There is no single place. The energy of each soul's every thought, feeling and free will choice throughout the lifetime is instantaneously registered in his lifeprint, and at physical death, that collective energy automatically draws the soul to the matching energy layer of Nirvana. It is there that the soul reviews his lifeprint, and since *only* that soul reviews it, there is no need for a central area.

S: Yes, I see. What happens to parallel lives when the original person dies?

MATTHEW: They can continue along their circuitous courses many more years, or some may have taken a route that already had ended the lifetime.

S: Since they have no bearing at all on the person's conscious awareness, what is their purpose?

MATTHEW: They do some of the emotional learning that is required of all souls for their evolvement. Hundreds, maybe even thousands of lifetimes may be required for some souls to learn just one essential lesson—say, generosity instead of greed—and parallel lives may be working on this one issue in their "series of events" in the continuum. The thought forms directed toward this multiple, simultaneous experiencing coalesce, intensifying the learning and eventually taking hold as a firm advancement of the soul growing in godly ways back to the Source of all life. So parallel lives do have considerable significance.

S: I'm confused, Matthew. Are different souls sharing parallel lives?

MATTHEW: No, Mother, those lives that started at the various pathway forks are different energy aspects of the same soul. Consider a house as the soul and all the electrical appliances in the house as the multiple lives of that soul. Only one wire from the source of electric current is needed to conduct electricity into the house, and once the current is present, all electrical appliances can be activated whenever needed because all of them have the same energy nature. In my analogy, gas or oil appliances cannot be activated because their energy nature is not electrical. In that same way, entities whose energy makeup differs from that of our subject soul could not operate within that soul's energy field.

S: Ah, now I understand. I've also heard the term "probable lives"—are parallel lives also called that?

MATTHEW: Not correctly, and in your concept of life, the term "probable lives" would not be easily understood because you don't think of *energy streamers* as having a life. But just as one thought form is a living substance, a number of thought forms generated by the same source toward a specific situation also have life. Probable lives are energy streamers that begin with your first thought about a particular situation and grow with each subsequent thought about it until you decide not to take action on whatever you had been contemplating.

The major difference from parallel lives, which function outside of your consciousness, is that probable lives fit into your conscious recognition. When you are considering a particular decision, you think about the *probable* result if you follow through to an outcome. Even if you make a different choice under the same conditions and circumstances, the energy of that original probable result remains.

S: Do the energies of parallel lives and probable lives combine after we initiate them?

MATTHEW: No, because of the differences in their intensity and levels of reality. Parallel lives are not in your awareness at all, but the possibilities that always precede probabilities and the probabilities themselves are a strong part of your consciousness. For example, you think about taking a trip, and at that point the trip is a possible result of your conscious consideration. With more thoughts about this, say deciding when and where to go, you add to the probable life's energy around the trip. However, until you actually begin traveling, your thoughts about "possibly" and then "probably" going were creating the energy that motivated your actions right up to the moment of embarking upon the trip.

The investment of energy in parallel lives works the same way insofar as starting as slender energy streamers and gaining strength and momentum in accordance with your decision-making process, but its stronger energy enables it to make its way without any direction from you and it continues on its own pathway, as I described. The weaker energy strains generated by your thoughts of possibilities and probabilities meander about until they play themselves out if you never again think about the situation that originated them, and the energy invested in them rejoins the neutral universal energy pool.

However, if your interest in that original situation continues and intensifies, those energy strains of the probable lives are correspondingly strengthened and influence your decision to follow through with decisive action—or not. If your decision is "Yes, I'll do it" and it is of such significance that it creates a fork in your pathway, you have just initiated a parallel life on the pathway you left behind.

S: Well, thank you for explaining all of that, Mash, but I can't begin to comprehend all those nebulous parts of my life. It's overwhelming trying to imagine my soul as a part of another soul, and that soul as part of still another and so on and so on and everything happening simultaneously.

MATTHEW: I know, Mother. In third density it isn't possible to comprehend that Creator is the exact same All That Is as before Its first creation, or that the countless subsequent souls eventually will reintegrate with All That Is, where all life in the cosmos began, is, and ever shall be. On a microcosmic level, it is the same with the personages, each with its conscious life, parallel lives and the influence of possible and probable situations.

I know that the indestructibility of energy and thought forms is the basis of all that is created, but please do not ask me for a detailed explanation of how all of this works—I don't know. I can answer some of your questions because of my vantage point in this realm and other questions because of our highly spiritually evolved sources here and beyond, but some aspects of the master plan are a divine mystery to most of us, too.

Souls far wiser and more evolved than I claim that the closer to the light we progress, the simpler and clearer everything becomes. We complicate life by constantly tapping into the universal thought forms and embellishing or trying to simplify them, thus attracting countless more of them to deal with. The expansion and contraction of All That Is cleanses, heals, reveals all the "mystical" parts of Itself, and holds the light-love all souls need for evolvement.

I do see the divine plan more clearly now than when I first arrived. It is a progressive remembering process, because souls' core "ingredients" contain all universal knowledge. The more we strip away the layers of forget-fulness, pretense and negativity, the easier understanding becomes and the closer to the light we return—this is the goal of every soul in this universe. To progress from one growth stage to another is as simple as living in honesty, kindness and harmony with others and keeping an open mind to enlightenment along the way. This you do understand, Mother.

S: Matthew, it's a much easier way to understand the purpose of life!

MATTHEW: Then let all the information that is not easy to understand lie quietly within your soul, where it always has been understood, and be at peace knowing the purpose of life.

UNUSUAL EXPERIENCING

S: After you told me about "dual lives" [a soul who has embodied on Earth and, for other types of learning, goes to Nirvana during the person's sleeping hours], *I thought of more questions about them. Do they account for child prodigies?*

MATTHEW: Indeed! This is true particularly in cases where the family history doesn't indicate that such a gifted child would be likely. These extraordinary achievers, especially known in the arts and the sciences, may have chosen genetic inheritance that also adds to their remarkable abilities, but even without that extra benefit, these geniuses are truly "heavenly" endowed.

S: Do dual lives affect savants the same way?

MATTHEW: No. Although this also is a chosen lifetime, like a prodigy's, this is an entirely different situation. Generally savants are remarkably gifted only in one ability, usually in music or painting or mathematics, and their other cognitive abilities are seriously compromised. Chemical mechanisms within the developing fetus affect certain parts of the brain; non-affected parts develop to an extraordinary extent, which severely retards development of the rest of the brain. If there had been no chemical imbalance, most likely the person's overall intelligence would be average or slightly above average.

S: Is autism related to dual lives?

MATTHEW: No, not at all. People are born with this condition, but it is not due to genetic heritage or birth injury. Autism is a self-contained experience the soul chose to counterbalance hyperactivity in another lifetime. I don't mean hyperactivity in the sense of an extraordinarily active yet essentially healthy individual, but rather a glandular malfunction that causes a person's inability to control the urge to be excessively active and vocal.

It is purely a matter of the soul's strong will that enables it to overcome autism's natural resistance to leave the sense of safety in its "cocoon." Environmental influences may either accelerate or stifle the autistic child's capacity to learn and become functional within what you would consider a normalcy range. Still, a positive environment in itself is only a buffer between the condition and the behavior, which would be far worse in apathetic circumstances where neither love nor assistance was provided.

The soul always is aware that this is a lesson it chose, and it feels only love and patience for its personage that agreed to experience that kind of lifetime. Those are the same qualities the person himself needs from his family for the most positive response to his life's challenges.

S: *Do souls choose to be born with physical or mental abnormalities or be brain-injured during birth?*

MATTHEW: Congenital abnormalities usually are provisions of the pre-birth agreement. Not only can the child progress spiritually during a lifetime with physical or mental challenges, but this fulfills a pact with the parents, who are the next most affected and sometimes *the* most affected by having an "abnormal" child. When these roles are in the family agreement, they are made prior to the birth of the parents. However unlikely it may seem that even before their birth, the parent souls agree to be mates and agree to limiting conditions that will affect their child who would not be conceived until many of your linear years later, all arrangements are made in the continuum where all souls are learning in simultaneous lifetimes and the matching up of all principals in the agreements is done.

In the case of a perfectly developed baby who is injured during the birth process, this also can be part of an agreement. When it is not, then it is quite another matter. If a potential birth injury is anticipated, the principal parties discuss this at soul level. If any one of them does not want to accept the possible turn of events, a new agreement prevents the potential birth injury by means of a miscarriage or stillbirth.

A new agreement also is required when there is an actual birth injury that was not part of the original agreement. The principal parties discuss this at soul level, and if anyone rejects this condition that none of them chose, the baby dies. If all souls agree to accept this unexpected situation and whatever will result from it, the baby survives and a new agreement is made that includes a different set of life circumstances for everyone involved.

When you consider that agreements extend far beyond any child and its parents—they include other children born into the family and all other relatives, people who will play important roles such as closest friends and teachers, the soul who agrees to later be the child's spouse and children born of that union—you can see that many lives are seriously affected when an original agreement is amended, and equivalent karmic lessons must be arranged for all those souls.

The actuality of living with serious limitations and the stress on the family may be considerably more difficult than the principals had anticipated in pre-birth discussions. When there are positive responses to the physical, emotional and financial adjustments inherent in providing optimum care for a person with special needs, family members can take leaps in karmic learning and soul growth, and perhaps healing. For instance, when there is loving caretaking, a severely mentally deprived person can experience the peaceful life he needed to recover from traumatic lifetimes.

Abusive treatment may or may not be part of a pre-birth agreement. When abuse or neglect is within the family agreement, all parties chose those roles to balance other lifetimes. But when abusive treatment was not chosen, it is the same as with all other situations outside of agreements: Persons who endure unchosen hardships can grow spiritually far beyond that point selected for the lifetime, and conversely, those who were neglectful or abusive incur karmic lessons that will result in serious counterbalancing in other lifetimes.

NEVER are physical, mental or environmental hardships a punishment from a divine source!

S: Why is there such a condition as insanity?

MATTHEW: When veiled memories of fright about the prospect of separating from the parent soul reach a person's consciousness, the feelings are so formidable that he cannot remember how to function as his DNA was coded. Those memories of despair, which are triggered by some occurrence the person can't consciously identify, catapult him back into his beginning moments as an individual soul and the primordial cry for understanding, vision and belonging. DNA coding exists in all embodied souls and those frightening moments happen to every individual at third density spiritual evolvement. Some feel that separation sensation more often and more intensely than others, and those who feel it most profoundly become what you term "insane," a mental state that prevents rational thought and functioning.

This happens to souls who long ago used their free will irresponsibly and wreaked havoc with their manifestations, and those cellular memories are carried forward in *cumulative* soul memory to all generations of personages. These souls are not being punished by Creator for the trauma they caused others, they are only reaping what they sowed and now are mentally captive of their manifestations. If they cannot accept the help of the lighted beings who attend them in each incarnation, each lifetime is another torment for them, and they will repeat and repeat and repeat. Please understand that it is the *soul* that is subjected to this history and not a matter of free will choices that causes the personage to act and react in the manner you associate with insanity.

S: *Did our races develop from different soul groupings?*

MATTHEW: It isn't a matter of different souls, but different ancestors. Most Earth humans are direct descendants of members of human civilizations who came to the planet and mated with either their own kind or the most evolved of the human root stock that they brought later on to perform heavy work. It was not the intent of the original populating program to vary the races, but when those who were in charge realized that several races contributed much more to the whole civilization than would result from only one, they continued the diversity.

Souls have lifetimes in every race, which differs only in appearance and developed characteristics and never is superior or inferior in soul essence or growth potential. However, some souls—especially those who incarnate in persons you call native or indigenous peoples—retain spiritual awareness in far greater degree than the rest of Earth's peoples of any racial descent.

Your current population is not the most advanced civilization to live on the planet. Except in rare times of Earth's history, many individuals have been far advanced spiritually, intellectually and technologically compared with today's residents, and they had superior health and beauty as well as much longer lifetimes. With Earth's rich human history, it is sad that many people now seem satisfied to believe their ancestors were apes.

CONSCIENCE, INTUITION, IDEAS

S: I know how conscience feels, but I don't know why we have it or how it develops.

MATTHEW: Conscience is the influence that each soul has on all of its personages, and ultimately, it is Creator's influence on all of Its creations that have the ability to think. Most simply said, the purpose is to keep incarnated souls on track with their pre-birth choices and to motivate souls in spirit lifetimes to keep evolving. The goal of *every* soul is reintegration with Creator. A cumulative soul needs all its personages to achieve balance in each lifetime so it can progress toward balance at the level of First Expression souls, where only the love-light essence of Creator exists. Without conscience, that "return home" journey could be never-ending.

Conscience is the component of the soul that is composed of light energy with fluctuating ability to signal "right" or "wrong" to the person who is deciding what to do in any situation. People who consistently ignore those signals make choices that unbalance their energy, and without balance their energy drops into densities far from the light. Because that removes their conscience from its light source, it ceases to function—when it is said that a person who has committed a heinous deed "has no conscience," that may very well be true.

There was no need for conscience until after Creator gave Its First Expression souls free will to manifest whatever they wished. Eventually it was realized that a "memory prodder" was needed to safeguard souls' awareness of their Beginnings or those memories could be irretrievably lost. So conscience was designed to peel off layer after layer of forgetfulness until total memory of The Beginnings is regained.

S: OK then, thank you. What about intuition and ideas—where do those come from?

MATTHEW: No single source. A few thousand years ago, when spiritual clarity was an integral part of Earth humankind, angels and their designated humans had a close relationship. Because of that closeness, those peoples lived many times longer than you do today. Now many on the planet don't believe angels exist, and some who do "believe in them" perceive them as ethereal beings playing harps in heaven. In either case, this wide separation from angels often causes individuals to disregard their intuition because it seems like unwelcome conscience, but actually they may be ignoring angelic advice.

S: So angels are the source of our intuition or at least one of the sources?

MATTHEW: I did imply that, Mother, but it's more accurate to say that they are part of one of intuition's two primary sources. The brain retains memories of every-thing you have experienced, and, like your computers' functioning, your stored information can be sorted and retrieved by triggering the proper keys. The "data output" for a specific new situation is all previous pertinent experience and knowledge, and acting on that is what you think of as using "common sense." That's one source of intuition.

The other source is beyond one's consciousness, the

"divine nudging" with each new experience, and this is where the angels come in. When a decision is required in a new set of circumstances, often it is angelic advising that influences the wisest decision about an action or reaction. After that experience, the knowledge derived from it is added to the brain's storage facility, ready to be used intuitively as "common sense" at the next appropriate time.

As long as the brain is functioning properly, the collective intuitive insights are the substance of the common sense pool of wisdom and knowledge that affects all subsequent actions. Once there is any brain deterioration, which can result from injury, illness, or the prolonged use of alcohol and other addictive drugs, all subsequent thoughts and actions are correspondingly debilitated.

Many people attribute all extrasensory information only to God or they think it's their own imagination, and that is the difference between the perception and the reality. That kind of information comes from many sources—God, angels, spirit guides, beloved ones in Nirvana, galactic and intergalactic beings, and some does originate within a person's reasoning processes. But when you consider the inseparability of all souls with God and each other, you can see that it really doesn't matter whether ideas come from Him or His many emissaries or your own mind—whatever the origin, intuition is the soul's messages to the consciousness.

KARMIC LESSONS

S: You said that we choose our lifetime karma, but it's hard for me to believe that all the people who are suffering horribly actually chose that, or that anyone would ever choose to be cruel. It seems to me that life is karma just tossed willy-nilly and the unluckiest people get hit by the worst.

MATTHEW: That's because you don't correctly understand karma, Mother. The soul's objective is to achieve balance, and karma is the provision of conditions and circumstances that eventually will bring balance to the soul's multi-lifetime experiences. The soul chooses its karmic lessons prior to each incarnation to fill the missing links—"the other side of the coin"—or to complete an unfinished lesson. Some lessons are very difficult to accept and endure, but not only easy ones can be chosen or the soul cannot grow beyond that point.

It is understandable that you see cruelty and hate it and pity those who are suffering, but you cannot know what underlies the actions. Just as I told you that homosexuality is an advanced stage toward androgyny, balanced male and female energies, the balancing of all other human emotions and relationships also is required. The "suffering" soul may be balancing its karmic obligations from lifetimes of willfully harming others and the "inflicting" soul may be balancing lifetimes as a "victim."

That used to be the chosen karmic experiencing of all souls who incarnated on Earth, but that is not the case in this unprecedented time on your planet. Many millions who are living in fear, devastating poverty, despair and disease are being deprived of learning their chosen lessons by the perpetrators of those conditions—persons who have fallen so far from the light in their abuse of free will that they have totally disregarded their own souls' chosen lessons. When causing pain to others is not part of a pre-birth agreement of all the souls involved, negativity is produced by both the perpetrators and the suffering ones, none of whom chose or need those experiences for balance. But you cannot consciously know whether karma is being enacted or ignored—that is why you are told not to judge anyone, but rather feel compassion for those who are suffering and abhor the circumstances that are causing it.

Karma is not only opportunities for souls to gain balance, it is a symbiotic relationship between souls and Earth. As microcosms of Earth, humankind add to her balance as they evolve through their own karmic learning, and this gives Earth more light to radiate to her residents, thus giving them a boost toward attaining balance.

Karmic lessons can be presented anyplace in this universe. Although lifetimes in other kinds of physical forms and worlds is essential to progress toward reintegration with God, then with Creator, usually Earth is the schoolhouse for experiencing all emotions incurred from the beginning of human life on the planet. When that is mastered, souls evolve into other life forms in placements where intelligence and spiritual awareness are beyond the present capabilities of the great majority of Earth's peoples. In your concept of God as "up," you can clearly see that intelligence and spirituality came "down" to Earth—it did not begin in the sea and rise to ground level.

S: For sure! What you explained does make karma more understandable—thank you. So apparently all of us do choose the same kinds of experiences in one lifetime or another.

MATTHEW: No, Mother, that's not quite how it goes. A soul has to counterbalance any sensory situation previously experienced, so the learning spectrum of emotions can differ. For example, if a person murdered someone, his soul would need a lifetime that ended by being similarly killed so it can feel the emotions of both a killer and a victim and achieve balance in that regard. If a soul has never been a murderer, no counterbalancing as a murder victim is necessary because those extremes do not exist in that soul's emotional spectrum.

S: How is the spectrum of emotions determined?

MATTHEW: They are inherited. The karmic lessons now being played out in your world were initiated in your ancestors long before civilization began on Earth. The extraterrestrial beings who populated the planet did not want their cellular memories of war to burden the new Earth humans, who had not experienced and perhaps would not ever need to experience such atrocities. However, only Creator can extinguish cellular memory, and the DNA could not be wiped clean of the ancestral memories. If those had traces of an originating extreme— the initiator of an extreme act that required a balancing act—those aspects of cellular memory were passed on to Earth humans as part of their physiological and psychological makeup. Since not all of the ancestors' history included battles in space, their progeny did not inherit those extremes.

Expressions such as "being born into sin" and "original sin" are not rooted in the extraterrestrial source of the karmic balancing currently underway. Those expressions are innocent misinterpretations or deliberate misrepresentations of what Earth humankind once knew about their ancestry. Now most of the population have no idea that millions of souls from other civilizations are surrounding your planet to help preserve its very life or that many are living among you, much less that "ETs" are your ancestors. I believe the Christians are not considering that in their concept of "the only Son of God," Jesus is an extraterrestrial being.

POLARITY, DUALITY

S: How did polarity and duality originate, and how do they fit into soul evolution?

MATTHEW: The forces of polarity emerged in deepest antiquity when some souls who felt they were superior beings started to dreadfully mistreat the souls whom they considered less than themselves. The lesser souls were newer, weaker God fragments and often much less mentally evolved than the more powerful souls who were abusing them. That was the root of cruelty and other forms of ungodliness in this universe, and because physical lives could last thousands of years in those early times, the brutality of the stronger souls and the pain of the weaker ones created a massive amount of negativity.

As more and more feeble souls were subjected to misery, the negativity kept building until there were equal forces of dark and light, or respectively, negative and positive energy attachments. Accountability was established so the weaker souls could reclaim their god-self heritage by returning pain to those who started it. The ultimate leveling process arrived at a division called polarity, stabilized energy opposites, with karmic learning opportunities at each end so balance could be attained. The powerful who mistreat the weaker in one lifetime, in another incarnation will be the frail ones who are mistreated by those souls whose "turn" it is to be powerful. Not reward or punishment, but reaching an energy balance is the purpose of this seesaw experiencing. The pathway to balance can span hundreds or even thousands of lifetimes as resistant souls get repeated chances to break this cycle, yet they keep failing because their free will choices continue to be rooted in negativity.

S: How does polarity affect Nirvana?

MATTHEW: The energy of souls' immediate past Earth lifetime automatically places them in the corresponding energy layer here, but the polarizing forces of their karmic lessons don't come with them. Different forces are here, different types of energy, but we don't need the lessons of polar opposites or the energy pattern established by polarity as you know it, such as the North and South Poles, the dark of night and light of day, or searing hot and freezing cold.

Unlike polarity, which is a universal condition, duality is within the individual, the range of opposing characteristics or attitudes that each person struggles to incorporate into a balance. Since souls arrive here in the same state of mind and belief systems they had on Earth and most lived by the duality philosophy, imbalance comes here in abundance, mainly in souls from Western cultures. The beliefs of Eastern cultures don't have that degree of duality, but they have their own distortions, and adherents to those philosophies also need to relearn souls' inseparability from God and one another. Balance is the aim not only of each soul, but the universe, and we cannot emphasize too strongly that duality is a powerful weapon of the dark forces for suppressing your innate knowledge of the light within balance!

S: How much does our balance increase when we transition to Nirvana?

MATTHEW: Just entering this realm doesn't increase balance at all, and living here doesn't automatically mean an increase, but this is a good place to work toward that because duality is more quickly overcome here than on Earth, where it is an asset to the mighty would-be conquerors in your world. Reincarnated souls can once again fall prey to those individuals, who are controlled by the off-planet dark forces, but that control is coming to an end in this unprecedented era in the universe.

Mother, these years at hand are extraordinary in many respects. There is acceleration of the time that you have devised as hours and days. Acceleration in divine grace being extended to souls who want to amend pre-birth contracts for earlier transition to spirit life or for other cogent reasons. Acceleration of karmic lesson completion. Acceleration of planetary cleansing assistance from advanced civilizations. Acceleration of light beamed from off-planet sources to restructure your cellular makeup so you can physically survive in fourth and fifth densities, where Earth is ascending.

These times of greater light forces' activity than ever before in Earth's history are evoking greater efforts of the darkness as counterbalance. The still-prevalent negative energy attachments, which cannot be destroyed, will be transmuted into the ever-intensifying light on the planet or transported to placements where negativity still is part of karmic learning. Polarity will not last much longer in your world—the opposites of "heaven" and "hell" on Earth eventually will be reconciled by the balance within light, the most powerful force in the universe.

PART IV

CREATION

THE BEGINNING

Ithaca, a free spirit who is the presenter of all information in PART IV, has been in Nirvana since her lifetime during the Inca reign in Peru when she was a sacrificial virgin. While free spirit can mean that not even an etheric body is required by a soul, in a different sense it is one's close communion with God and the conscious awareness of the pre-birth chosen mission— only the latter applies to Ithaca.

As the ancestor soul of many residents of Nirvana, she is a spiritual inspiration to them; because of that connection as well as her teaching and healing service, she is loved and honored throughout that spirit world. Her important services also have entitled her to remain there an extraordinarily long time.

I felt Ithaca's vibrations as gentle and lilting, reminiscent of a lullaby. This musical quality makes her energy especially valuable in the healing of newly transitioned souls whose Earth lifetimes were lived in or ended by traumatic circumstances.

In the image Ithaca sent me, she was wearing an elegant oriental silk costume and her shiny black hair was styled in that traditional fashion; her complexion is Oriental, and her gently slanted dark eyes softly radiate love. Her appearance surprised me, as her last Earth lifetime would seem to indicate quite a different one. Matthew explained that due to Ithaca's esteemed service, she had been granted refinement of her last embodiment's coarser features and sturdier figure into the more delicate countenance and petite body she favored.

Matthew and Ithaca share a special kind of love, and with Esmeralda, a Mexican child who entered Nirvana as a toddler, they are a family.

The Council of Nirvana requested Ithaca to give the following presentations for this book. Although some of Ithaca's information will be familiar to you via Matthew's explanations, her manner of speaking is sure to delight you.

Before the beginning there was nothing we can know about, and then there happened a great explosion of such intensity that it cannot be imagined. It was the self-expression of Creator Mind, which had existed until that moment silent and motionless. Into the previously unknown came light so intensely brilliant as to be its own radiance.

That moment was the manifestation of Creator's silent idea to share Its total knowledge and power and presence with all subsequent expressions of that original essence. It was not only sharing, it was actually parts of Creator that came into being in that first moment. Nothing existed before then, and everything that has existed since then has come from Creator, the Source of All That Is.

After Its contemplation to experience through shared life in energy form, Creator first manifested the highest angels. The emergence of that angel life is called First Expression, and those first children of Creator are called the archangels. The essence of Creator was not diminished by creating children, but only shared with them, just as your essence is not diminished by your children, but only shared with them.

In Creator's love for Its children, It gave them free will with its indivisible ability to co-create with Itself whatever manifestations were of the souls' own choosing and ideas. Manifesting at first produced nothing visible except to the Mind of Creator. It was totally a mental process accompanied by what we could call emotional awareness. Simple in theory, it also was simple in the beginning efforts when all consciousness was close to Creator.

Possessing all the powers and capabilities and knowledge of Creator but on a smaller scale, the archangels mastered manifesting instantly because there was no separation of their minds and the Mind of Creator. With Creator, they created the next realm of angels, not quite as high in the light but proportionately still possessing those same elements of knowledge and power as the archangels.

Within those angelic realms there was recognition of the inseparability from Creator and each other because the same creational material was the essence of all. Manifestation was then still only in spirit form, pure energy in love and light. Without division between the Creator and the created, there was only harmony and shared love. That was the original intention of manifestation.

Then, into those stages of cosmic growth came denser formations. Most dense in form were the celestial bodies of the universes and least dense were the beings who went forth as gods or goddesses to rule over them. All of those souls had proportionately the same power, love, knowledge and intent of Creator. One of the gods became the ruler of this universe, and this is the Supreme Being whom many of you call God. Using His co-creative powers with Creator, God became the maker of all life within this universe.

As the layers of creating continued and the density

deepened away from Creator's light, bodies of substance were required and the first manifestations were perfect. Only perfection could result in those beginning stages because the universal bodies and the incarnate beings were made within the shared mind and intent of Creator.

As eons passed, the brilliance of love and light that was Creator-in-sharing became dimmer spiritually in the lower layers of manifested entities. Those lower, denser layers came into being because inherent within free will was the total freedom to choose what to manifest. That included the choice to do harm as well as good, and what happened is this:

Into the light Archangel Lucifer had given thanks for his creation and expressed this in manifestations that still lie in the highest realm near Creator. But Lucifer became more and more curious about what all he could manifest. Since manifesting is simply making something from whatever materials are available, it is possible that a lack of experience may produce something quite awful and far from intent. Or, there may be a deliberate intention to create something horrible. Lucifer did both.

Outside of the mind and intent of Creator, Lucifer and his angel followers at first produced dreadful bodies due to their inexperience. But soon they found delight in this, and experimenting with mating substances to produce grotesque beings became their intention. With each layer of deliberate abuse of Creator's original intent of free will in manifesting, Lucifer and his adherents fell farther and farther into the morass of spiritual darkness.

You have heard of mythological half-human and half-animal creatures with ungodly bodies but with the power to think. They were actual creatures in deep antiquity, made from the combinations of human and animal mating materials, but through the passing of time and change, the truth of their existence became the legends of mythology. Lucifer and his band of fallen angels made those creatures.

Some were designed out of pure meanness alone and were meant only to be horrors with intelligence, such as the ferocious and hideous dragons on land and in the sea. Others were designed to be functional, to perform work on the planetary formations in various places in the universe. For instance, the half-man, half-goat, which was able to run swiftly and carry a load on its back yet had the ability to reason; and the intelligent mermaids and mermen, who were made to carry out experiments and other labors beneath the seas.

From the power and glory and soul goodness of the angelic realms, Lucifer and his band had chosen to fall into those depths of depravity that allowed such deviate and cruel manifestations as the miserable animal-human beings they made in abundance. Long ago having ceased to be angels, Lucifer and his group had fallen so far away from spiritual grace and attunement with Creator that they became captive of the dark energy they themselves had created. Their base energy would not allow their ascendance back to the light from which they had come.

What happened to Lucifer and his followers was not punishment. Their descent into the captive darkness never was the wish nor intent of Creator or God, who could only honor the free will of those fallen children and beam love into that dark energy their choices had created.

Life in our universe was made in the love and light energy of God manifesting within Creator Mind, and the laws of the universe have been in effect since the first moment of life formations. One of the primary laws is that the farther from Creator Source, the denser the energy, and the denser the energy, the darker the surroundings because the distance in allegiance to Creator and alliance with the light has become so formidable. By the universal laws, our universe could not be free of the cosmic effects of that Luciferian dark energy.

Never has the darkness in Earth human nature been decreed by Creator or God as punishment! It is but the atmosphere of prevailing dark energy influences into which humans are born. Each infant comes with the light of total purity in God's gift of life. It is through free will and the exposure from birth onward that each soul may see and follow the light or may align with dark forces and be influenced in that direction.

And so it has been to this day: God honoring all of His children's choices and beaming His love and light throughout all lives in His world.

ORIGIN OF EARTH HUMANKIND

The story of Adam and Eve had its roots long before it was recorded as the biblical genesis of human life on Earth. It is a story that has captivated many otherwise searching minds, minds that stopped thinking at that legendary level that defined the development of Earth and its human life.

Without unfolding the layers of mistakes in interpreting universal Beginnings and subsequent occurrences, there can be no truth unfolded, either. It is necessary to unwrap the many untruths so energy alignment can take place for ascending into higher realms of understanding and higher frequencies for spiritual awareness.

Ostensibly, all religions originated their own dogma to benefit the peoples. But in fact, accurate historical recordings show that a few people who wished to control the many peoples deliberately devised falsehoods that enabled this control. Very long ago the religious leaders made up stories to confuse and mislead the minds searching for an understanding of their Beginnings.

The leaders saw that the truth would allow people a closeness to God that did not require money or intervention by other humans, and that did not suit their purposes. So to satisfy their greed and desire for control, the leaders contrived layer upon layer of distance between God and the individual heart and soul. It is their false information that you revere and hold most sacred.

Worshipping God is not kneeling and feeling lowly, it is looking within and exulting in the knowing of one's inseparable God connection. And church is not a building.

Church is completely within each soul! The very earliest churches were the only ones in accordance with God's intent. As explained by your biblical Jesus, when two or three souls gathered to worship in God's name, that was showing glory to Him and therein He would be found. Never was church intended to be a structure, using materials and labors to honor a God increasingly removed from conscious communion. But the diligent and reverent beings who followed the dictates of the self-serving few fell under the spell of the mystery, and soon all truth of one's direct and constant spiritual connection with God diminished almost to extinction.

The deliberate distortion of God's truth is not part of your biblical history, but there is evidence of that fact from records found in caves and tombs. Divinely inspired translations of the ancient languages and depiction of those records were given directly to specially chosen individuals, but those translations have been suppressed by the same dark spirit that was behind the origination of the lies.

The Sumerians, as the third civilization on Earth was known, had preserved a modicum of truth about the origin of the planet's human life. Because they did not survive long enough to spread this information so broadly that all Earth inhabitants could have the same explanations, many legends came about. But the basis for the legends is too deeply entrenched to be totally obscured, and it shows a kindred understanding of the true origins and purpose of human life on this planet. And that true history is this:

Prior to human development on Earth, souls elsewhere had evolved to a far higher degree than current Earth peoples can imagine. Those more highly evolved humans were the lesser gods and goddesses and the major mortals of planetary habitations within this galaxy and well beyond. Through their amazing intelligence they designed technologies, including space travel, unknown to you today.

At that time your planet belonged to God Himself, and there was a beauty and simplicity and perfection that indeed was a garden of Eden. There was a need in this solar system for such a planet, with ideal conditions that would engender health of spirit, mind and body, and where human intelligence could be imparted and nurtured. "Eden" was derived by transposing the letters in "need," a word created prior to any human life on Earth. Much later, that word and its definition were introduced and preserved in the English language.

Into that uninhabited paradise came powerful groups from Lyra who wished to extract gold from the planet, which was called Shan by the civilizations living during that era of evolution in the universe. The Lyrans had thought to arrange an exchange with the inhabitants of Shan, but they found none with whom to discuss any such consideration.

In violation of universal laws, the group had gone to Shan without clearance from the Intergalactic Council. Further, they did not petition the Council for mining rights. They meant to hide their discovery of this paradise, which was a literal gold mine, from other civilizations also using that metal for technological purposes.

Thus greed, deceit and disobedience came to the planet in negative energy before Earth humankind was introduced. The biblical interpretation is the first man being born into sin through the depiction of the serpent tempting the first woman with a fruit of this Eden garden. It is necessary for you to know the origin of the interpretation that is your story of Adam and Eve.

Those greedy, deceitful Lyran visitors were the originators of some of the later inhabitants of Earth. Their reason for bringing to the planet her original beings was as simple as this, slave labor. The Lyrans felt that for such a purpose no human status with a God connection was necessary, and they brought high-status animals with an instinct for following orders. That introduction of such beings was the beginning of the genetic makeup—the human root stock—of the earliest ancestors of Homo sapiens.

Eventually released from slavery, the embryonic human population flourished in bands in the most habitable lands in the continents now called North and South America and Africa, and in the Middle East regions. Planetary land and sea masses were much different then. As climates changed and as food abundance lessened, the groups migrated to other lands for survival. They developed over many periods, now known as the Pleistocene epoch, some of them called Neanderthal and Cro-Magnon in their evolutionary journey.

At a designated point of evolvement the beings were ready for seeding, which was a mating program to initiate the intelligence and spiritual aspects that would elevate them to fully defined HUMAN status, H(igher) U(niversal) MAN. At the time of the seeding, extraterrestrial humans came to live among the primitive Earth beings. They were from different constellations, thus providing the genes that produced the varieties of body shapes, skin colorings and facial features of current Earth populations. Due to the cohabiting of these extraterrestrials with the Earth population and the direct implantation of intelligence through that genetic structuring, the thinking, reasoning, conscience-endowed Earth humankind came into being.

Theirs was not the ordinary evolutionary process.

They were endowed genetically with an intelligence factor that evolved in a time span of only about 30,000 Earth years, a uniquely rapid time in your time structure for any profound development. The DNA containing the intelligence quotient was immediately reproduced in the seeding, thus quickly enhancing development of the Earth human brain.

Thus it can be clearly seen that humankind as represented by Adam and Eve did not spontaneously appear on Earth. Nor did humans descend from the apes as theorized by Darwin. There was a similarity only in ancestral physical form, with approximate sizes and upright movement. All varieties of the ape family on your planet diversified from the original ape root stock. Humankind evolved into current likeness directly from the parallel developing of the human root stock introduced by their extraterrestrial ancestors. The brain and God fragment with soul attachment introduced directly and ONLY into Homo sapiens is the vital difference in the two lineages.

At the juncture when people had advanced in intelligence so that Earth human minds were completely separate from their extraterrestrial ancestral minds, there came also a departure from their inheritance of spiritual knowledge and God connection. While intelligence continued to increase at the rapid pace intended, the original spirituality became entirely lost. With that loss, Earth humankind erred in its pathway to understanding its origins. The level to which intelligence had been developed was lost as well and never has been restored.

Those forces of darkness that led people astray from their spirituality now hold fewer souls captive as many of Earth are hearing and heeding the voice within to look upward to the stars and not down at the "sinner's feet of clay" idea that has been foisted upon you. Soar in your oneness with the eternal wisdom and love of All That Is. You are part of that vastness. Let it be so.

LEMURIA AND ATLANTIS

The "lost continents" of Atlantis and Lemuria are not fanciful stories. They are part of Earth civilization's beginnings, and most souls embodied on Earth today were part of those two populations during their most turbulent times.

Atlantis stretched from the east coast of current United States across a portion of the Atlantic Ocean and was contiguous with the continent called Africa. The remains of this vast continent lie beneath Atlantic waters. At ocean bottom in an area of your Pacific lie the remains of Lemuria, or Mu. Lemuria included what is now the west coast of the United States and about half the area of the current Pacific Ocean. In some places the former continent connected with the land mass that later was jolted far to the west and today is Asia.

The seas known today as Atlantic, Pacific and Indian Oceans were smaller at that stage of planetary configuration. Originally Earth had more land surface than water, but not in areas that would be recognizable today, and water covered areas that now are land masses. The many island groups in the two major oceans today were formed from the massive changes initiated by the destruction of those two "lost continents."

The combined populations of Atlantis and Lemuria at their peak totaled approximately your population worldwide today. About 50,000 years ago, long before the nomadic tribes of biblical description, great civilizations with highly developed cultures, technology and longevity of physical life lived on the two continents.

Both intellectually and spiritually, they were attuned to
God, the lesser gods and goddesses, the higher mortals
and each other. This is because their ancestral seeding
program had furnished them with both intelligence
capacity and awareness of their oneness as fragments of
God, inseparable from All That Is and each other.

At the height of those civilizations, technology existed
far beyond what is now known on Earth except for some
types of weaponry and computers. Particularly the leaders
of Atlantis had become obsessed with technology, which
called for ever-increasing intellectual development. This
obsession with mental power became so exclusive that
over time all memory was lost of their spiritual nature
and their direct linkage with God. All knowledge of their
origins was lost. That loss, combined with the focus on
mental intensity, allowed base energies to enter and
entrench themselves in the hearts and minds of those
people. It was their willful separation from God that led
to the end of the civilizations that once flourished so
grandly on Atlantis and Lemuria.

There is an explanation for all major happenings in
the evolution of our universe and this profound Earth
happening is no exception. When the memory is lost of
one's soul connection to all other souls and to God, the
weakness that is created can be exploited by the base
energies that have existed ever since the angelic realm
divided into light beings. Some of those beings later
became what you call "fallen angels."

The fallen angels lost their power to create life in
conjunction with God, and they never had the power to
create life without God. Therefore, they have to use
existing bodies to experience in physical form, and so
base energies always are looking for entities that are
devoid of awareness of their oneness with All That Is.

The unaware entities consequently are lower in density, which makes them easier prey for the dark energies to enter and control. Many such individuals were among the leaders in Atlantis and Lemuria.

From technology that could have been beneficial to the entire civilizations, there came instead to some minds an interest in using weaponry to control the peoples. The use of crystals was well known in those times, including for that purpose. Atlantean scientists developed the ultimate weapon, which mis-reacted to its designed usage and caused an implosion of the vast continent as destructive as many simultaneous nuclear explosions.

The devastation was massive. Earthquakes and volcanic eruptions were set in motion on the landmass that had not already separated and sunk beneath the sea. Two lesser destructive phases followed before that continent's total disappearance, where it still lies in gigantic divisions on the floor of the Atlantic Ocean.

The cataclysmic end of Atlantis was a chapter of human history repeating itself. Ten thousand years before, Lemuria was destroyed in similar fashion, by the harnessing of the power of crystals for destructive purposes.

There were no survivors from those two mammoth planetary upheavals. All peoples disappeared along with their continents because of loss of faith, loss of memory of the Beginnings, loss of spiritual connection with the Oneness. Into such a gap in the integrity of Earth humankind eagerly had come the planet's ancient contaminants of greed, power and relentless pursuit of avenues away from godliness, the components of negativity from deep antiquity. The negativity could not remain or Earth herself could not survive, and thus all human life had to be done away.

THE GREAT FLOOD

Millennia passed with barrenness on your planet before its repopulation by the same celestial ancestors of those peoples who were lost along with their continents. In time, this new civilization fell into the same malaise of spiritual awareness as had Earth's previous residents and they, too, forgot their Beginnings. Once again the forgetfulness led to increasing inclinations to play in the darkness, and once again it became necessary to rid Earth of the negativity that was caused. The destruction of life and the repopulating came again, with similar results.

There came such a flood that almost all of the planet was covered with purifying water. However, this time it was not meant that all lives would be lost. You know of only a few of the survivors through the biblical story of Noah and the ark. Many other places on Earth besides Mount Ararat gave refuge to humankind and animals. Most of the surviving peoples lived in outlying areas, away from the sophisticated populace. These simpler peoples had not lost their spirituality to the degree their leaders and many others had, so in them was preserved the seed of their Beginnings and spiritual bonding with God.

While some beings followed their inner voices and migrated to higher areas, others stayed where they were as their inner voices assured them of safety. Still others were rescued by their ancestral beings who had conducted the re-seeding program. In all instances, the survivors had preserved their awareness of the God fragment within each, of the interconnectedness of all souls, and of the reunification that would be the end of each soul's spiritual journey through many lifetimes.

When the waters settled, the peoples started adapting to the changes in Earth environments and within human consciousness. The scattered groups slowly increased in numbers for many centuries. In the biblical story of that period, only the part of the population ascribed to Abraham and David is mentioned, but that was only one of many descendant segments of survivors of the Great Flood. And, as time elapsed, they lost much of the spiritual awareness that had enabled the survival of their ancestors.

Eventually the civilization increased and scattered until there were both settled and nomadic populations in many parts of the world. Along with this arose food and water shortages and favored locations, and with those conditions emerged the warrior temperament. It became in some minds necessary to strengthen their own groups through conquering others. Remembrance of origin and inseparability from the God source was lost to almost all the descendants who lived in areas now called Europe, Asia and Africa, and factions of those peoples were frequently in combat for domination. Ironically, conquests and slavery became most commonplace in those populations considered "civilized."

There did not exist such harshness of character in many of the descendants in the areas now called North and South America. Those peoples developed a legendary explanation of their connection to the Great White Spirit or to gods as remembered in dreams and visions of the extraterrestrials who had come to save them. While such remembrance was not confined to those peoples and peacefulness did not characterize all groups in the western hemisphere, it was most prevalent among those populations.

It is of note that the people who were rescued by their extraterrestrial ancestors did not lose touch with their origins, but nurtured them in their legends, while those who survived without extraterrestrial assistance entirely lost all awareness of their Beginnings.

And thus Earth humans have evolved unto this day.

THE BERMUDA TRIANGLE

Forces we could only call neutral, because they are neither for nor against human life, are now at work and within a few years can cause great changes in Earth's configuration. A major area involved is your Bermuda Triangle, about which are many stories of mysterious loss of planes, boats and people. The mysterious disappearances are not due to climactic conditions, which is one explanation. There is no UFO base beneath the water, as some theories hold.

What is in that location is an energy vortex that is the reawakening of Atlantis. The energy comes from an immense crystal, the one used in the weaponry that ultimately caused the disappearance of that continent. This crystal is the most powerful force field on your planet.

No sinister purpose is behind the loss of the travel crafts and lives. Simply, when they entered this dynamic force field, they entered into a space beyond Earth's third dimension. Dematerialization of the affected people took place, and once out of that frequency, they were re-manifested in their same forms. Some physical lives were lost when extraterrestrials were not in the vicinity to save them, but many of the people who disappeared did encounter those rescuers and are living in their same consciousness in another dimension of being.

PART V

VIEWS OF EARTH
AND OTHER
WORLDS

VIEWS OF EARTH

S: Matthew, what do you see when you look at Earth?

MATTHEW: It depends on how I look. With full sensory viewing, I see red and purple jagged streaks of light racing around the planet and other streaks shooting up from the surface—red is anger and purple is spiritual awareness, the opposing energy forces that are struggling for balance. What I see in that kind of viewing is the collective emotions of all life on the planet as reflected by Earth herself, who is a sentient soul and the composite of all the energy attachments generated by her animal, plant and mineral kingdoms.

When I look at the planet without full sensory viewing, I see haze and distortion—this is energy swirling in the negativity that is so destructive to Earth's very life. Nothing in this haze, even the land and sea masses, is evident as an individual form.

When I focus on something specific, regardless of size, I can see it very clearly. Not as you would see the same thing, but as it is with its energy attachments. My love of flowers hasn't changed, so it is with joy that I see your hillside of wildflowers in the purity and vibrancy of the energy their beauty and simplicity are creating. I can see the flowers more clearly when I'm with you in spirit and most of all when I am there in my etheric body.

If we visit in spirit only, our visibility range is limited. We're not limited in feelings or our heart and mind connection, only in vision as you know it. Our sensation of beauty is just as keen when we're present in spirit, but we see finite details more clearly when we're there in body.

My long-range viewing is not limited to Earth, but being able to observe the planet from this distance to the point of seeing you life size is a wondrous visual journey! Both that visual capability and my going to visit are astral travel, which can be actually traveling in etheric body or simply visioning from here to there.

The other side of focused viewing from here is not as lovely as the wildflowers. For instance, I see oceans clearly only in places where pollution has not damaged the energy flow. These are the saddest places on Earth. I see animals exactly as you do, but also I see them beyond the limits of your vision. I see some as glittering, radiating their gentleness, and some are so dense that they're just dark globs. This is sad for me, too, because they're not "bad" animals. They're only following the natural predatory instinct that was bred into them by the dark forces, and the energy of that instinct is registered as the dark glob.

IMPORTANCE OF CETACEANS

S: Why did you say the oceans are the saddest places on Earth?

MATTHEW: Because they are the home of the whales and the dolphins, the most intelligent and most spiritual souls on the planet, yet their homes have been defiled by intention and carelessness, and their inhumane treatment is an indelible mar in the nature of Earth's human civilization. Cetacean energy is as sacred as human energy insofar as individual and collective souls, but their homes have been gravely polluted and their lives brutally ended.

S: Matthew, did I receive that correctly—did you say cetaceans are more intelligent and spiritual than humans?

MATTHEW: That's what I said, Mother, but I should have stated it more precisely. It is species-wide that cetaceans are higher than humans in spiritual and intellectual attainment. I didn't mean that never has any human on Earth achieved or exceeded that level. Some exceptional humans have—certainly Jesus the Christ and Buddha the Christ are exalted above that high level.

You may remember when we were talking about Earth animals coming here and I said the entire whale energy on Earth doesn't come, only enough to create the human-whale energy bonding. The rest of that pristine life force goes forward in spiritual growth after its Earth service, and their souls transition more rapidly than humans through this realm on to planes of higher vibrations, or evolvement.

S: *That's quite a revelation, Matthew! Recently I heard that some whales have shown what seems to be an interest in friendliness with humans. Do you know anything about that, and does it have any significance?*

MATTHEW: Yes, I do, and yes, it has major significance. The whales' activities that signify less fear of humans is evidence that the increasing light within human consciousness is lessening the influence of the dark forces on the planet. That influence fractured the human-whale energy bonding and permitted the mass slaughter of whales, and even though the power of the darkness is waning, it still is motivating some individuals to treat whales as only profitable commodities.

The cetaceans' intelligence and spiritual evolvement was once recognized and respected by Earth's peoples, but that disappeared from conscious memory as the energy bonding between the two species was relentlessly attacked by the dark forces. In addition to stimulating humankind's capacity for brutality, the dark forces wanted to completely eliminate whale presence on the planet and they influenced humans to do their dirty work. Whales anchor light energy beamed at Earth from distant sources, and their holding pattern of that energy within the ocean depths and vastness is at a wavelength beyond the dark forces' attunement level.

If the whales were gone, so would Earth's major means of anchoring light energy be gone, and without an anchoring source, the light cannot remain steady. When light cannot be dependably maintained, its power ebbs and flows, and it cannot attain the intensity or scope required to strengthen Earth's life force. Only if all anchors of light on Earth were extinguished could the light itself be vanquished, and only then could the dark forces claim the dead planet as their prize. That planetary death would have come long ago if extraterrestrial civilizations had not directed light energy to Earth and the whales' anchoring power held it steady. Their service was essential not only to preserving Earth's very life, but enabling her to ascend into higher frequencies and be restored to her former health and beauty.

Earth is more than a small planet in an ordinary solar system in a minor galaxy among the billions in our universe. The planet was one of God's favorite placements and actually was the paradise named Eden. Its radiant aura and pristine beauty made it a showcase in this part of the universe, where it was a testament to the power of God co-creating with Creator in love-light energy. The planet then was the antithesis of all that the forces of darkness had made to plague the universe, and the conquest of Earth became their objective.

Now you can see why influencing her humankind to eliminate whale life has been one of the major strategies and a goal of the dark forces. To counter that negatively-aimed energy, some humans have acted on soul level inspiration to bravely and steadfastly work to save the whales from extinction. The current comeback in whale numbers is specifically to raise vibrations during these years of Earth's ascendance out of negativity as the light heals her planetary body and lifts the consciousness of her peoples.

MORE ABOUT ANIMALS

S: Do animals evolve?

MATTHEW: Yes, lower animal life forms evolve into higher animal life forms. By and large there is a pathway that animal energy follows in its spiritual and intelligence progression, and even minute insect energy travels from point A to point Z in its growth. Animal energy doesn't always embody in animal form, but it can do so for many lifetimes while learning to recognize its value in the Oneness of All. Creator's light essence is the source of all manifesting energy, and just as human lives are sacred and inviolate soul-selves, so are the lives of all animals.

Each animal soul comes to Nirvana after its Earth lifetime ends and, like a human soul, it chooses its next embodiment based on its past lifetime experiences. As an animal acquires greater intelligence, it also gains awareness of the inseparability of all life and the direct connection of all with God and Creator.

This is no less true of the few species whose current instincts can't be adapted for living in this realm, as the rest of animal life can. This is not about animal evolution, but the dark ones' cruel experiments that deliberately created ferocity in the animal kingdom. Although creational energy comes from Creator, intelligence and spiritual awareness is a different matter—it is the intention of the designer of any life form that generates and delineates its energy usage.

The fossils uncovered on Earth by no means represent the only animals that lived there long, long ago. In the very beginning of animal life on the planet, all species had a mild and mannerly nature. Later, due to vile experiments as the dark forces abused free will, animal design fell into lower density where ferocity could be manifested and sustained. The creation of the first fierce specie destroyed the animal energy balance that had been prevailing within the light, wherein all is balance. Once the polarity of fierceness and gentleness was established, the "natural enemies" concept formed the two extremes in animal natures. Although the creatures developed by dark intent aren't in your recorded history, some of them are depicted in mythology as grotesque monsters on land or in the sea.

The dark designers didn't confine their horrible creations to huge animals. They also made fleas, for instance. Fleas always were meant to be only an abomination, ranging from annoyance for the animals they infest to the diseases they initiate or spread. An even more harmful intention was behind the design of the tiniest life forms, the microbes, whose purpose was to create havoc of immeasurable impact among all other life forms.

In their evolution, some animals may have a human soul source. Although most do not, some in the higher orders may derive from a human soul that wishes to experience as an animal to fill a niche in the growth pathway that such a life would enable. If so, usually the choice would be among animal species that most often are treated with mercy and caring rather than those who are treated miserably or are raised only for food or whose lives are untouched by humans.

I'll give you an analogy of how a soul can direct an energy stream to initiate an animal—or human—lifetime. Think of the soul as a pond into which you toss a pebble and see how sun rays upon the rippling water create countless points of light. The refraction of light and the energy in the ripples represents human soul energy streams that may be used to manifest any number of animal and human lifetimes, whatever the soul chooses to achieve balance. All of this takes place in the continuum, where all those lifetimes are happening simultaneously.

S: How interesting! Can the energy of animals on Earth be tracked the same way humans' energy can?

MATTHEW: Yes, indeed! As the myriad thoughts and feelings "shoot" out from Earth, we know which come from animals and which from humans. And just as with human identification, each animal is known by its unique characteristics that are registered energetically in what could be compared to a bandwidth or a brightness factor.

I know this will please you, Mother—your dogs have a guardian angel. The angel in the canine domain has chosen your dogs to receive the love and care that is universally known about you and Bob. None of your adopted "fur kids," as you call them, came to you by accident, but by reward or compensation to them. It is the same with all animals and their loving caretakers who are "led" to each other.

S: How wonderful to know this! So then, all pets have an angel?

MATTHEW: Yes, and so do those animals you might not consider so lovable. There is an angel for each species through a soul level attachment, not an individual assignment such as humans' angels have. These special angels are ancient souls whose beginning was as animal life when all animals in this universe were peaceable, spiritual and intelligent beings.

At soul level animals are aware of the angelic benevolence on their behalf. Even those whose lives are miserable have an angel force or influence to ease discomfort or end terribly painful physical lives. Some angels have greater numbers of animals or more intelligent ones to protect than others, but no specie's angel's responsibilities are more important than any other's because all of those lives are meaningful in the universal balancing of animal energy.

The angels bring a sense of unity to their respective animals to preserve the species, but it isn't their prerogative to wipe off the face of Earth those humans who are cruel to individual animals or even an entire species. Environmentalists who are acting in good faith—that is, not for selfish political, personal or economic reasons— are being inspired in their efforts by the animals' angels.

S: How severely has Earth been affected by species' extinction or near depletion?

MATTHEW: There is no simple answer to this, Mother. The cause of death of even one animal and the effect cannot be separated when measuring the negativity involved. Long ago the extinction of all animals on Earth was due to a profound and abrupt change in climate, but their mass exodus did not result in negativity. It was a swift event caused by Earth's need to release a vast accumulation of negativity that had been created by the brutality of people who were unaware that they had fallen so far from God's truth. Nevertheless, the result was drastic—obliteration of ALL life on the planet and the need to repopulate. In some cases, the new life forms were quite different from previous residents.

Now let us address a more recent situation, the North American bison that roamed by the millions until, in a short period, almost all were wantonly killed. Some were shot merely for sport, but a darker intention was to eliminate the life-sustaining resources of the continent's native population. In this case there are two measures to consider. The killing was rooted in vile intent, thus producing negativity. The massive loss of animal life also raised a huge cloud of negativity; however, that was transmuted into light because the innocence of the lives lost counterbalanced that sad happening and there was no lasting negativity. But the abundance of negativity created by the vile intent behind those deaths did remain.

The destruction of animal life due to ignorance or unintentional neglect or injury also has a counterbalancing effect that doesn't produce lasting negativity. That is not true when the killing of an animal is a merciless, torturous act by one who derives enjoyment from such depravity. Despite the innocence of the animal, the negativity created by its pain and torment plus the negativity caused by its tormentor, DO last. Consequently, just one such killing produces tenfold more negativity than the mass slaughter of cattle or swine or poultry for food. Even though this may seem to you to be disproportionate, the intent of the latter kind of killing is not rooted in malice. Although in most instances the killing methods are inhumane, the purpose is to provide human nourishment and this gives counterbalanced energy.

Another example of counterbalancing is animal use for medical research. While this surely is not merciful treatment, the experiments are intended to benefit humankind by finding ways to treat or eliminate diseases. Therefore the negativity produced by the anguish of the animals is offset by the intent of the research.

But, sadly, there are many more examples of animal treatment that DO produce lasting negativity. All killing of whales, of course, and the vast destruction of dolphins and other marine life due to willful carelessness of fishermen. The animals subjected by humankind to loss of their natural habitat and food supply. Those who are sickened, killed or malformed by deliberate pollution of their environment. The animals who are killed for their fur or tusks, eggs or fins or other body parts, or who are killed only to be stuffed as trophies. The domesticated animals whose owners deliberately neglect health needs or starve or beat them. In all of those cases there is lasting negativity from the combination of the cruel or greedy intentions of the perpetrators and the energy of the animals that live and leave Earth in terrible desperation.

There are other types of animal treatment that produce undiluted negativity. The psyches of animals confined in zoo cages are traumatized. How can anyone not realize that this existence is torturous for animals accustomed to roaming free, many in family groups, and then forcibly taken from that life and confined to a cage? We do see that there is innocence on the part of the youngest spectators, but the energy they give forth does not counterbalance the negativity created by the pain of the animals in confinement.

The encouraging aspect of animal capture for display is that in some zoos, spacious environments natural to some of the animals are replacing cages and outdoor pens, and breeding programs have been initiated to preserve species near extinction. In the case of "performing" dolphins and whales, some people have been inspired by spirit to recognize the grave harm that captivity causes these beautiful souls and to strive to make more acceptable homes for them. However, only a few of the multitudes of your confined animals have been liberated by these means—the vast majority still are suffering horribly in their captivity. It is the same cruel existence for circus animals, which not only are physically maltreated in many cases, but are psychically crippled by their confinement and unnatural use for human amusement. In none of these situations is there a counterbalance to the immense negativity caused.

The tortured psyches of all of those animals need healing time in Nirvana just as traumatized humans do. When you consider the millions upon millions of animals who suffer those various fates I mentioned, you can see the extensive efforts required here to heal them all.

Mother, I strayed from answering your question, but what I've just told you is vital for people to know so the horrible treatment of Earth's animals will stop!

Now then, back to your question. Anytime an entire species is completely or nearly obliterated, certainly there is a planetary effect, but because counterbalancing transmutes negative energy into the light, the change may or may not be harmful. What may happen is a "domino effect" from humankind's disturbing the balance Nature had achieved.

Let us consider the effects of insect extermination, by far the largest number of animal lives destroyed, however with little lament. When crops are widely devastated by insects, this unbalances the energy in people who suddenly face hunger or at least financial considerations. Chemical extermination stops the pests' destructiveness and allows crops to flourish, thus relieving concerns about insufficient food and lifting the negativity of those concerns. However, the domino effect of the "solution" produces other circumstances—the surviving insects are hardier and resistant to the chemicals and there are concerns about the impact the chemicals have on human health.

When the human factor enters into the balance that Nature has established, even with good intentions sometimes it creates more negativity than it eliminates. So, you see, Mother, there is no simple way to measure the impact on Earth that has resulted from destruction of her animal life. But it is safe to say that a lot of the negativity that so adversely is affecting your planet is directly due to humankind's pervasive disregard for animal life.

AURAS

S: Bob and I are wondering if you see us exactly as we appear to each other and if you hear our voices the same as we do.

MATTHEW: I can hear your voices as you yourselves do and I see exact images of your physical appearance. I also see your energy fields, your auras, where you appear mostly as a light, shimmering, fluctuating being and Bob looks more solid. You appear like that, Mother, because you are more sensitive, more easily touched by emotional situations than Bob is. He is more dependable in his outlook, approach and progress in a situation than you, and that accounts for his more solid appearance.

S: Well! Is there any significance to auras beyond this differing in appearance of our emotional makeup?

MATTHEW: Oh, yes! Auras indicate where you are in your spiritual growth in this lifetime, and not everyone has an aura. It depends upon whether there is enough light within the soul essence to be reflected through the physical body. The souls we call "lost" are so trapped in the density of negatively-bound energy that they have no light ingredient at all for an aura, not even for a visible outline.

The aura contains every possible vibration within the person, from joy to sorrow, wellness to disease, tranquility to fury. When you react strongly to someone of differing nature, your aura registers a light that clearly shows a readiness to defend something so basic to you that you cannot tolerate another perspective. I don't mean simply differing opinions, but differing convictions or principles the magnitude of opposing sides in a war or zeal in any controversial issue of major importance, like religious beliefs.

SEEING THE FUTURE

S: Matthew, how do you know what's in my future or anyone else's?

MATTHEW: We can see symbols registered in energy form in what you could call one's personal field of potential. Depending upon their intensity of momentum, the various symbols can be categorized as possibilities, probabilities or certainties, and they can be projected into a "future" situation, as you would think of it. Actually, individuals already have set that "future" in motion with their thoughts, feelings and actions, and the energy that those are directing will likely follow a particular course.

Location, health, finances, education, job changes and more, I'm sure, that I'm not thinking of in this moment, are quite easily projected because the energy that is invested in "probable" developments can be easily tracked. The more private, or personal aspects of life— such as increased spiritual awareness, improved discernment ability, enhanced job skills, development of talents, greater intelligence usage, and wiser judgment— are harder to project due to changing sources of influence. Relationships also are difficult to project because of the many variables that may be created by either or both of the participants.

Channels of personal information—individuals you call mediums, readers, psychic intermediaries or seers— lump all of that energy in motion in a person's field of potential as possible developments, and they address the range of possibilities to fit the requester's specific questions. I'm not a seer or a source of information for one, and I'm not an expert in interpreting the symbols, but I know it is the degree of that interpretive skill that distinguishes a "clear" channel from one who means well but hasn't developed that expertise.

Mother, when I tell you of situations you inquire about, first I discuss my impressions of what I see with someone here who is keenly adept at symbol interpretation. This is a learning process for me, but what you will appreciate more is that I am confident about what I relate to you.

S: Thank you for that! How does a channel obtain someone's personal information?

MATTHEW: The person's desire to know something in tandem with the channel's ability and willingness to assist form a reciprocal energy pattern that accesses the person's lifeprint in the Akashic Records, where all information about his life is registered in the symbols I mentioned. So the channel has the person's history in addition to the current circumstances he has set in motion in his energy field of potential.

Channels also can contact sources who furnish information directly or who act as intermediaries—that could be the channel's spirit guides or the person's own guides, family members or close friends in this realm or any other being who is knowledgeable about his life or other lifetimes that are influencing this one.

The finest of all channels are the very highly spiritually evolved souls who can tap directly into the universal consciousness, but they are rare indeed. Mother, the individuals who spoke for me during the years prior to our personal contact were of that caliber. It wasn't as you thought, simply your good fortune to find them—you were led by our energy bonding to those whose consistency in reaching light sources and receiving clarity I already knew.

Psychic ability is one thing and spiritual clarity is quite another, and the two levels of attainment may differ greatly. Without spiritual clarity, channels cannot access spiritually evolved beings, but they may not know that their sources are not within the light. Channels who formerly did have spiritual clarity may not realize that because of undue stress, they have dropped from their high energy level that was compatible with their evolved sources, and they continue to believe that the information they receive is from the light when it is not.

Illness, fatigue, physical pain, grief, self-doubt, anxiety about the circumstances of dear people, and financial worries are stresses that take a heavy toll on a channel's energy level. If they don't know that any of those conditions has resulted in their reaching less well informed sources, and possibly even dark entities, naturally they believe the information they receive is accurate. Channels who fall into an "ego trap" automatically reach low level entities because the negative energy of egotism isn't compatible with the energy of light. If they don't realize what has occurred, they don't know that the information they are given and pass on is from dark sources.

Many individuals with varying degrees of psychic ability who advertise themselves as mediums are far more interested in their clients' money than in providing them with accurate information. Along with tapping into their psychic abilities, such individuals cleverly elicit clients' comments and weave both sources of information into a seemingly likely "future." Motivated by greed and operating with wiliness, they have no possibility of reaching spiritual sources and their information cannot be trusted. And then there are the complete frauds who merely claim they are channels and, like the "borderline" psychics, deviously elicit information from unsuspecting clients and weave it into some palatable "future."

Mother, it is with good reason that many people are skeptical about channeled information!

WAR AND PEACE

S: Will there be a nuclear holocaust by intention or accident?

MATTHEW: Creator and God will not permit any activity that would endanger souls anywhere in the cosmos or cause the destruction of Earth, and both would be the certain outcome of a nuclear war on your planet. Creator's sole exception to Its law that all souls' free will must be honored is that never again may anyone wage nuclear war. If the dark forces persuaded Earth individuals to start such a war, God-appointed intergalactic forces would prevent those darkly-influenced persons from following through with their intention. The same technological intervention would apply if nuclear warheads were released by error.

Souls have been shattered in nuclear type warfare among earlier civilizations. Damage to the "ingredient" of souls that is their equivalent of bodies' DNA is the greatest devastation possible, and the souls who suffered this damage are changed because of it. When a soul is shattered, the "DNA" that holds the original memories, which may span many hundreds of lifetimes, is scattered in parts throughout space. All the parts must be located, reunited and the memories of each integrated into the soul that must be reconstructed.

The parts may have infiltrated a body anywhere in the cosmos or be drifting in free spirit status, and as they are discovered by search teams who are aware of the soul's shattering, they are guided "home" to join the other found parts. Finding, then integrating all the parts, which is a healing and restoration process, may require eons or may not even be successful, but the attempt is essential because the soul must be fully restored before it can reintegrate with Creator. Souls whose reconstruction is unsuccessful or whose parts cannot all be found are absorbed into Creator's essence, and the individuality and experiencing of those souls is lost. So you can see why the incalculable damage that nuclear wars have caused never again will be permitted.

S: Yes, but I can't understand why that exception to free will pertains only to a nuclear war. Why isn't the desire of the vast majority of people for PEACE honored and ALL wars prevented?

MATTHEW: The conflict is between light and dark forces, and all souls within each force are exercising their free will. Honoring only the desires of people who want peace is in effect denying the choices of the people who don't. Not only would that be "taking sides"—by Creator's law, that isn't possible anyway—but it would not allow individuals to follow the course of their chosen lessons in pre-birth agreements, because at this point in Earth's evolution, wars are offering them opportunities to complete those third density lessons.

There's another consideration here, Mother. Those people you say "desire peace" may indeed not like war, but is their focus intently on peace? Think of the numbers in military forces, the workers in the many industries that directly support war, and the people in the many businesses that provide auxiliary services to all those others. Those millions and millions of people may not consciously advocate war, but their financial base is dependent upon war-related occupations and they have enormous energy invested in the continuation of their livelihood, thus the course of their combined energy is toward war, not peace.

So you see, a situation may appear to you to be clear-cut, but within universal laws, it is much more complex than you realize.

JUPITER'S SURPRISES

S: Did the comet really strike Jupiter as just reported or hasn't the full story been disclosed?

MATTHEW: The intensity of the comet's fragments in their direct hits is much like your scientists reported, but no report or scientist has all the facts. Jupiter has seas of desolation, and some of the largest pieces of the comet hit those areas where no life was endangered. The caretakers of the life forms were able to manifest directional influences, but not to the extent that no fragments would hit the planet.

Contrary to the conclusion of your astronomers that Jupiter is an immense uninhabitable gaseous orb, it has a non-human population numbering in the billions. Beyond your telescopic range exists an atmosphere that sustains life, where seeding projects of both animal and plant life are conducted. While many of the life forms are microscopic, little more than benevolent bacteria in nature, in some cases the experimental animals are as large as horses, and in great quantity they are as small as a pigeon. Some of the animals have functioning brains beyond the instincts inherent in their DNA. To answer the question in your mind, Mother, yes, DNA is the root of every life form throughout this universe.

Jupiter is somewhat like a galactic nursery as the animals that are bred and nurtured there later are transported to placements that sustain human life in this solar system and other parts of the galaxy. Most are used in the food chain, some are working animals, and others have pet temperament. Many types are unusually beautiful, such as the birds with brilliant plumage, exquisitely decorative fish, and the animals with brightly-colored fur coats. The symbiotic relationship of all the animals and the ornamental and food plants through inhalation and exhalation of elements that fortify and sustain life is the key to their flourishing on Jupiter, just as on Earth.

S: What a surprise about Jupiter! Who develops and takes care of the animals and plants?

MATTHEW: Both human and suprahuman beings, and the latter are unusual life forms themselves. They are suprahuman in that they have a brain function equivalent to sixth level density intelligence factor, but they are not necessarily that advanced spiritually. They are "neutral" in emotional makeup, hardly varying a millimeter off dead center of an emotional measuring stick. They are spider-like in shape and almost gelatinous in substance, with oval-shaped heads, and their unblinking eyes are huge in comparison to the size of the head.

So I've been told, these beings are Sirian in origin, but they have not been contacted for ages by the master planetary group council. Since they can breed and reproduce biologically, they don't use cloning technology for themselves, but they do in their animal and plant life experiments. They have lived on Earth for short periods universally speaking, but in your time for millennia, to introduce new animal species and assure that the weakest varieties were strengthened or removed.

Dinosaurs were the result of the largest land animal experiments ever conducted on Jupiter. Their appearance on Earth was about 60 million years ago in linear time, later than your calculated time of their disappearance due to a drastic planetary climate change. That change had to precede the introduction of many other kinds of animals that wouldn't have had a chance of survival had the dinosaur population still been around. No animals or plants ever have been brought to Earth without a marked change of climate preceding it.

The dinosaurs were considered a triumph in size, but the brain was never the principal target of the experimentation process, and the result was a featherweight brain capacity for the immensity of the body. In that sense, the experiment was not considered a crowning success, because a smarter animal in immense form was the aim. The body mass drew the strength as well as the energy to keep that strength supplied, and the brain development went backwards. The heads were not originally designed to be such small areas for housing the brain, but during the evolutionary process, that is what happened. Dinosaur experimentation did not continue because in terms of the longevity of animals' food chain and the breeding of healthy replications, it was considered more valuable to focus on other aspects of animal development.

S: Matthew, where did you get this information, and how do you know it's reliable?

MATTHEW: It's definitely reliable information, Mother! Why would you think that something that significant would not be known here? Just like many other things I've told you that you find hard to believe, that knowledge is fairly commonplace here and elsewhere. One of my friends, Hugo, has spent many lifetimes on Jupiter and has told me a great deal about his work there, but before I knew him, I was well aware of that planet's animal and plant development. It sure shoots down that theory of all life on Earth originating right there in the sea, doesn't it!

∾———❦———∾

HUMAN CLONING

S: Maybe—well, probably you know that a sheep has just been cloned and some folks are saying this could lead to attempts at human cloning. What do you say about this?

MATTHEW: Mother, you would be amazed at all I could say about this! Cloning is a relatively new process on Earth, but elsewhere in the universe it has been used for ages to keep civilizations from dying out. Furthermore, cloning is not as new in your world as publicly announced—adult humans have been reproduced by this process for some time.

S: Matthew, are you completely certain about this?

MATTHEW: Yes, Mother, I am. I've mentioned my friend Hugo. Because of his work with the plant and animal life on Jupiter, he's very familiar with cloning. I don't mean that he is the source of my knowledge—the reality of cloning is widely known except on Earth—but if you would like a thorough explanation of the human cloning process, I'll ask him to tell you about it.

S: Please do.

MATTHEW: Mother, Hugo is here in response to my energy beep. Go ahead, Hugo.

HUGO: Hello, Madam Suzy! I am glad to join your

company in this moment. It is my understanding that you have questioned if cloning of adult humans has been done on Earth. Indeed that is fact, and has been for some time, as Matthew told you. I shall start straightaway, at the beginning of the cloning process, if I may. Thank you.

Human cloning is a process whereby the cellular material of a living being is taken for the purpose of reproducing the exact same likeness in a new entity. The cellular material is placed in a sterile vial in a liquid conducive for the growth of that material in purity and without imperfections entering the substance. After it divides and subdivides, the matter is transferred to a larger laboratory container under the same sterile conditions and temperature and light controls.

The embryonic form becomes quickly apparent and soon the definite form of a fetus is easily recognizable. When the fetus has reached the stage of approximately six months of normal gestational age, it is transferred again, to a holding tank wherein the liquid approximates the amniotic fluid in the womb during pregnancy. In this liquid the fetus continues to evolve normally as if in a womb. When the fetus has reached term development, it is removed from the fluid and is then treated as if birth by natural means has occurred. Except, of course, there is no umbilical cord to treat. Minor cosmetic surgery remedies that absence of the normal appearance.

The process in human replication does not take nine months. It is accelerated by means of chemical additives and ideal circumstances of laboratory makings. The initial process can take between six and seven of your weeks for certainty of perfect fetal development, and another eight to ten weeks is required for the full growth. Since none of this is by natural birth processes, regular gestational time has no meaning.

Cloning is not confined to reproducing infants who are permitted to grow normally from birth into adulthood. When the clone of a specific adult is at stake, the period of aging from emergence of the infant into an adult in prime years, say between 30 and 35 years of age, is only between 350 and 400 days. About one additional month of aging is required to produce a clone of a 65-year-old individual. That is the approximate age of most humans being cloned on Earth at this time.

The substance that permits this rapid aging has not yet been discovered for such a purpose except by those few scientists engaged in the cloning process. A few individuals on Earth have been afflicted with a chemical imbalance that causes their bodies to age far more quickly than what is normal there. A 10-year old child can have the aged appearance and organic functioning and processes of a very old person. Old by your standards, that is, not elsewhere. The chemical that causes the imbalance in that diseased child's system is what is used almost to perfection in the process of rapidly aging infant clones into adults.

This aging acceleration process also requires the addition of several key nutrients to the diet and ideal laboratory conditions of temperature and controlled degrees of oxygen and carbon dioxide. The disadvantage is that when the appearance must be identical to the original person who is about 60 or 65 years old, then the entire cloned being must be aged until that identical appearance is reached. There is no way to stop the aging of the organs and still achieve the necessary appearance, thus the organs are subjected to all the stress of the accelerated aging as well as any deficiencies inherent in the family genes. Even if the newly cloned individual initially appears fresher and younger looking than the original person or the predecessor clone, it quickly breaks down and starts showing more advanced signs of aging in all respects.

I have spoken so far only of the body of a cloned individual. The brain is another matter. It is the most intricate aspect of the growth procedure, both in vitro and once in flesh. The human brain is a computer, and the downloading function from the original brain to the brain of the clone works exactly like your computers in this same type of process.

Duplicating the original brain can be done with perfection in an infant clone. Education is supplied continuously to the clone throughout the aging period from birth to adulthood, and the brain functions as normally as you would expect within the accelerated learning faculties. Because the brain is so vast in capability, the clone's absorption of information during the educational process is not only easy, it is most interesting for the people involved to see such giant leaps in learning. We observe this from here and see this as the only aspect of scientific nature on your planet that is beginning to be enlightened as to functional human brain capacity.

Madam, the extended educational process is necessary because an abrupt insertion of intelligence and knowledge on a "blank slate" would produce a neurological shock.

The clones are instructed from infancy by tutors who are specially trained behavioral scientists. This aspect of the process is exactly what you do with your infants, teaching them to become aware, alert, responsible little individuals with personalities, skills, a sense of responsibility and engaging mannerisms. The tutors, whose students are quite more unique than most, are trained themselves by personal films of the family and are supplied other intimate family history, thus they are familiar with all speech and movement mannerisms of the cloned individual.

It is another matter entirely when a swiftly produced adult clone is the object. A major reason aging can be accelerated is the brain's capability to absorb information and perform functions at a far faster and more comprehensive rate than most Earth people realize. In fact, if this were not so, adult human cloning there would not be possible.

In a rapidly-aged clone, keeping the integrity of all knowledge gained during the original being's lifetime to that point is at stake. The adult clone's initial memory ability is compromised to the extent that the clone may appear befuddled or momentarily at a loss for words until the memory kicks in or the clone's own thinking aspect overrides the hesitation and covers, so to speak. Since this is not highly unusual in "real" people, it is not generally noticed with suspicion in the cloned beings, but rather is considered only a human imperfection.

The downloading of all information in the brain of the original person or of the clone being replaced must be done at the moment of the need for the new clone. This can be done most successfully from the person's brain to the first clone. Slight deterioration occurs with every successive downloading procedure from the outcast clone to its replacement. No, the original brain cannot be used to circumvent this deterioration, even if that individual is still alive, because that original brain does not have the same accumulated knowledge as the most recent cloned entity. You can see that the identical store of latest information is essential if the replacement clone is to be accepted as the real person.

While we are pleased to see this advancement in technology on your planet, its misuse neutralizes our elation at your discovery. Powerful people are being cloned now and have been cloned for many years, and none of this started with good intent. Always it has been for control purposes. Some of your world leaders were cloned many years past and by now are in the thirtieth or more versions of the original person. The purpose of cloning those people is to create the certainty of their longevity and maintenance of their influence.

You can notice the abrupt and considerable change in appearance toward vibrant health and youthfulness of some world leaders as seen in TV films or photographs. Usually this high robustness and stamina immediately follows a day or a few days of absence from the public eye after a period of increasingly evident aging appearance. You attribute those remarkable differences to the person's brief vacation or recovery from a proclaimed illness, but here it is known that, simply, a new clone has replaced the old one.

Yes, several clones are produced at the same time, educated as I previously explained, and kept in various places on your planet to be ever ready as needed for the up-to-the-moment knowledge insertion process. Many versions of the clones are necessary because the art of this science has not been perfected on Earth. The cloned adult bodies disintegrate far more rapidly than same-age bodies having grown old naturally. This is due partly to the accelerated aging process from infant to adult body and partly to the lack of skill in those scientists who perform the various procedures. Earth's third density atmosphere also is a factor.

S: Hugo, excuse me, please. Well, thank you for

answering the questions that keep popping into my mind. But are clones accepted by the person's family? Surely they must be aware of what's going on.

HUGO: The cloned individual's family members are, of course, aware of the existence of the clone or clones, and they participate in both the educational process and the "cover-up." If they resist, they themselves are cloned, usually against their will, and their clones carry on with public functions. In some cases the original persons have died naturally, or they have been killed if it served the purpose of still more powerful people. Others are still living, although never seen in public. Only the clones are seen publicly.

To quiet your mind of its question, Madam, five countries have developed the cloning process with just about the same level of success with the reproductions, and one other country is still experimenting with earlier stages. Laboratories are designed around the same functional basis, with little variation in the overall process. Some years ago there were enough variations in procedures so that differences in the quality of the clones were easily detectable. The aging process was the primary difference in approach at the different laboratories, and there were consequential weaknesses in the maximum achievable degree of physical stability and brain downloading success. With the eventual agreeable exchange of technology so that all areas of imperfections could be improved, all the current clones are emerging with approximately the same functioning abilities, appearance and aging characteristics in all countries where they are produced.

Now to continue. I shall address the very important matter of a soul in a cloned body. As for a soul being or not being in these man-made bodies, most definitely, no soul is "born" in a cloned individual, but a soul may choose to enter one. There is good reason for a soul to enter, just as there is good reason for a soul not to.

For a soul who has been waiting to experience in physical form, it is an opportunity to do so in these waning days before great changes within God's plan for raising consciousness of the planet and all of you who are receptive. However, any soul who enters these cloned bodies knows the risk of becoming trapped by the dark forces that have pervaded the psyche of the original person and any predecessor clones. This is a particularly important consideration as brain functioning deteriorates with each downloading process, as I have mentioned, and thereby weakens a soul's mental resistance to becoming trapped. Also, in later versions of the clones, longevity is not long, so those bodies are not looked upon as the paradise life one might suspect of an individual in a highly influential position.

Why would any soul take on such a problem? The power of such an influential position is exactly why some souls are not only willing, they are eager to enter the clone. They do so with the determination to overcome the genetic structure, the influence of the memory, and the inherent tendency to follow the negative path that the original soul was on. When a soul is very strong indeed, there is the will to uplift the genetic and moral character to the point that there does seem to be a turn-about in the "person's" health, attitudes and activities. In such cases, it is because the stronger soul's higher intention attracts the higher light energy that enables it to infuse the cloned body with physical stamina not available to those souls with less resolve, and therefore the stronger soul can sustain the body's life force for a much longer period than a weaker soul can.

Now you are thinking, how can any body live without a soul? The chemical makeup of a physical body is such that it is an independently functioning entity. Its life force is sustained by its own energetic momentum derived from the elements and interacting processes of normal organic functioning. Therefore, a clone without a soul has the same mobility and thinking capacity as any normal body.

Let us address what is not in a clone without a soul. First, emotions are not the givens they are in a naturally created human. A soul-less clone has to acquire the appearance of emotions in accordance with its surroundings, perhaps what is expected of a "regular guy" or maybe a member of high society. It is only conformance to the circle in which the clone moves that gives it the appearance of having emotions.

But the most essential lack in a clone is the spiritual aspect that is inherent in a baby born from the egg and sperm of its parents. The soul life force encompasses those aspects of being that are the bonding with God—conscience, intuition, sense of self at a higher plane than normal conscious functioning. So, neither those ties with God nor natural emotions are within the soul-less cloned individual. Instead, there is a mechanical and mental aspect of what is appropriate to do or say. Once mastered, that ability is as proficient as if the "person" had spent a lifetime accumulating wisdom and behaving properly.

Your mind is so full of questions, Madam! No, producing what you call "test tube babies" is not in the least the same nature as cloning individuals, and most surely not in purpose.

S: I'm sorry about thinking of so many things to ask

you, Hugo. Since it's public knowledge that a sheep has just been cloned, do you know why people en masse haven't questioned whether the same can be done with humans?

HUGO: Well, Madam, I'd say that even though the cloning of the animal is known, there will be no sustained information on that accomplishment. The art of cloning has not been perfected there, and the products will not age in the same normal way naturally-conceived animals do. When this is realized, there may not be many reports on it. Also I'd say that concentrated publicity could logically cause all thinking individuals to extrapolate that achievement into the possibility of human cloning. That kind of speculation does indeed exist there, but to prevent the major populace accepting such a feat as a possibility, much less a validity, science fiction in books and films is the masterful means whereby the human cloning technology is confined to entertainment, and always in a tenor of absurdity.

S: Thank you for your opinion, Hugo. What do you know about the aliens called "little grays"?

HUGO: Well, Madam, respectfully, we know all there is to know about them. With pertinence to Earth, we know that in underground laboratories, primarily in your Southwest United States, they are using their genetic material to reproduce themselves. When they arrived on Earth several decades past, they taught the cloning technology to your government-selected scientists, and that was the introduction of cloning to your civilization.

Ever since those beings arrived there they have done

little except misuse their high level of intellectual and technological abilities. They had not intended to remain long, but they became trapped in Earth's density and realized that they couldn't leave the planet because their systems no longer were of the higher density from which they came.

To keep their strain pure and to guarantee numbers sufficient to survive any attempts to exterminate them, they have been cloning themselves at a great rate. No, Madam, not exactly an army, as combat is not their immediate intention, but an army in numbers, yes. There is vastness in living areas underground on Earth that citizens would find incredible if they could become aware of it. It would be equally astounding if they could know that non-Earth beings are permanent residents on the planet.

These beings you call "little grays" are considerably smaller in stature than Earth humans and indeed look like the depictions given by individuals who were abducted for medical experimentation and reproduction purposes. Some of them are responsible for the abductions that took place as claimed, but with two huge and vital exceptions: where the kidnapped persons were taken and by whom. Trapped on the planet, the abductors no longer were extraterrestrial to Earth, and their travel crafts went down underground, not up into space.

These "extraterrestrials," as mistakenly cited, have not been anywhere except in the immense city mazes beneath Earth's surface since their arrival about half a century past. The only exceptions to their underground living are those brief abduction happenings. Then, using small spacecraft of their or your government's design and fabrication, they obtain humans to take back to the underground laboratories built specifically for their experimentations. These experimentations are in the nature of establishing a suitable mating program of the two civilizations, which, in the eyes of the "little grays," would reinforce their chances of survival on your planet beyond their pure strain by cloning.

Your major world leaders would like everyone to fear *real* extraterrestrials. They have considered producing the "little grays" in such aggressive exhibition that it would prove their stance that public fear of "extraterrestrials" is justified. Those leaders know that nothing is to be feared from the extraterrestrials in this part of the solar system! If it were not so desperately self-serving and so negative for Earth, to us it would be amusing that the United States government lets that mean-spirited alien civilization hide and experiment under your ground at the very same moment it denies the presence in your skies of representatives of civilizations they know are benevolent.

All space brothers in your area are friendly and have let this be known to government leaders. Most are there expressively to SAVE your planet! Cooperatively, they are preventing Earth from losing orbital regularity and are assisting you in myriad other ways. This service in universal friendship has been ongoing for many years and will continue during the heavier cleansing episodes ahead. Nevertheless, official statements continue to explain away sightings of the authentic extraterrestrial spacecraft by "logical" means.

Such foolishness, such childish games! But the consequences have been tragic for those space beings who some time ago came only in peace and offering technology and other assistance to preserve your planet. In exchange, they asked the world leaders to cease building nuclear armaments and planning for nuclear war that would destroy the planet. The government leaders would not give up their dark control, and they killed or held in captivity those peaceful emissaries. Despite that, those emissaries' fellow space beings STILL are helping you!

S: Hugo, I don't know what to say except that I pray our current leaders will be influenced by the light Matthew said is being beamed here. Can we go back to cloning, please—do you know when and why it started?

HUGO: I cannot tell you when cloning first was done, but the technology is in the universal mind and therefore accessible to those who tap into this ultimate source of all knowledge. I can tell you of a civilization that instituted this method of reproduction as a means of population preservation, if you wish.

I see your interest. Very well, then. That civilization's reproductive organs became atrophied due to disuse during an era of underground living after warring situations destroyed their planetary atmosphere. Limited space beneath their planet surface meant no increase in the surviving population could be allowed, and over great time their bodies changed to adapt to this new circumstance.

Their bodies had no cellular aging programming as Earth humans do, and that is why they didn't die, as you are wondering. When they learned that finally in safety they could re-enter their planet's atmosphere, they also realized that their few numbers would eventually expire to extinction if birth processes were not developed for sustaining the civilization. So, cloning came to the rescue as purposeful, pure and effective.

S: That is fascinating! Thank you, Hugo. How do you know so much about cloning?

HUGO: I studied it for the purpose of using it on Jupiter. Many animal experimentations are ongoing there continuously, and it is in connection with my scientific work that I have learned these methods of reproduction that include human cloning.

I am known in Nirvana mostly for relating the history of the formation of Jupiter and its subsequent animal and plant experimentation. As Matthew has told you, I spend most of my incarnate lifetimes on that planet. I'm not one of the large insect-like beings he described, but I do incarnate on Jupiter in a shape other than this etheric body you are now seeing.

I know Matthew said those individuals are rather strange, and he is not incorrect about that, but he is not as correct about their being emotionless. He is just unaware of the emotions that are deeply hidden within those beings due to their isolation from other civilizations. They are emotions that don't "rock the boat," in your term, so maybe they aren't noticeable to observers.

My people and I are not suprahuman, as those other caretakers are. I don't possess the high degree of intelligence development as they, but I have progressed beyond them in other ways by living in this realm between my incarnations on Jupiter. I am here now for learning more of the spiritual nature so that when I return—yes, I wish to soon return—I will have this additional knowledge of spiritual growth to share with my people there.

The last time I was on Jupiter was about 40 years ago in your counting, and I have been here since that lifetime. Yes, this is longer than most souls stay in this realm before embarking on new lessons. I had a great deal to learn so that not only my growth, but those I will teach by example, will be shifted toward the light more and more. They wish this, yes, Madam, otherwise my efforts would be worthless.

S: Hugo, does God approve of cloning?

HUGO: I am amazed by your question! I never thought to question this. I suppose He doesn't disapprove, as anything that creates for the higher good of the universe surely cannot be considered "bad" by God. It is in the abuse of this cloning capability, like anything else, wherein God most surely would be disappointed, I would think.

Madam Suzy, I ask respectfully that you return to discuss this matter with me another time. I shall come directly in response to your summons or Matthew will contact me, if you prefer. Thank you for this graciousness, and by this I shall say goodbye for a brief time.

S: I look forward to our next visit, Hugo. Thank you for all your information today. Goodbye for now.

The following day:

HUGO: Madam Suzy, thank you for receiving me again. I am heartened to tell you that cloning is not inherently against God. No, not at all. I have given this considerable thought since you questioned it. I have talked with one of the master council members whose wisdom in spiritual affairs is higher than any others in this realm, and he has agreed that cloning is not against

God's wishes, only the misuse of the cloned individuals or the self-serving purpose behind the development of them.

So, my reply rests more easily within me now, as I did not want to obscure your contemplation with my own opinion, which you might give more weight than deserved. Never is it correct to assume that because words come from here they are indisputable. We only have a vantage point you do not and the great wisdom of our masters for amplification of our knowledge.

I have enjoyed your company, Madam Suzy. It has been my pleasure to assist you in this way. If you have other questions later, you can contact me directly, if you wish. Now I bid you farewell in the leave-taking of myself into other good works and I wish you all blessings in your book preparation efforts.

S: Goodbye, Hugo. Thank you for your extra effort on that God approval point and also your good wishes. Matthew, hello again.

MATTHEW: Hello again yourself, dear soul. Hugo knows of your great appreciation even beyond your words because he picks up your feelings just as I do. His wish to return after consulting with a master teacher to give you that extra insight was extraordinary.

And Mother, his patience with your mental questioning yesterday also was extraordinary. I know you can't help those spontaneous reactions when you're receiving information that fascinates you, and I know you can't relate to the nuisance of your thought forms that just keep shooting up and distracting the concentration of the transmitter, but it's like trying to conduct a seminar in the midst of Fourth of July fireworks!

S: Well, I hope Hugo also knows that I can't help having questions pop into my head! Do you know how those people feel about being cloned?

MATTHEW: The few people who hold positions where cloning is usual welcome knowing that in the event of an incapacitating condition or sudden death, their power and influence will continue via clones of themselves. When the first clone receives downloaded knowledge from the person's brain, only the potential of being cloned is registered. Since the downloading procedure from the first clone to the second and the same with all subsequent clones does not carry "I am a clone" knowledge, all of them also know only of the potential.

S: How often is a clone changed?

MATTHEW: It depends on the individual. Usually cells are taken from a person only after he or she has attained a powerful position, and if this is after considerable alcohol or drug usage or the onset of a disease, the body is past optimum condition for obtaining healthy cells, so the clones deteriorate rapidly and require frequent replacement. Mother, you have commented to Bob about the remarkable difference in appearance of some well known government official or diplomat compared to just a few days prior, when that person appeared haggard and far less articulate—that difference is a new clone.

As Hugo mentioned, he sent me an image of himself. He is a most appealing young man with a wide, open smile, glowing white skin, dark sparkling eyes, and a shock of dark brown hair.

2008:

HUGO: Madam Suzy, how delightful that I am in your thoughts and thereby may join you at your computer! How may I be of assistance to you this beautiful sunny day, possibly by answering your questions?

S: Hugo! What a lovely surprise that you're here—it's been 10 years or so since we talked! Apparently you know that I'm wondering if clones will have any place in Earth's Golden Age.

HUGO: Indeed I know you are wondering that, which is why I am at your service. The need to use clones for the continuity of power is rapidly lessening as Earth approaches the promised era of deliverance from darkness. However, we are happy to report that the few cloned individuals that were entered by souls strong enough to overcome the dark orientation of the cloned persons are thriving. The souls' light and determined spirit produced healthy minds and bodies, and these people are dedicating their lives to serving your world in positive ways.

S: That is good news! So I'm right in thinking that there won't be any need for cloning here when Earth is in the Golden Age?

HUGO: Yes, and part of the revelations leading to that era will be the truth about the decades of cloned leaders and the dark purpose behind that.

S: From occasional Internet articles I see, some people already are aware of that.

HUGO: We see this too, of course, and you rightly surmise this is evidence of higher consciousness in those people, but still for the population as a whole, this will come as quite a shock.

S: *Along with many other truths! Hugo, are you still in Nirvana?*

HUGO: No, Madam Suzy. I returned to Jupiter two years ago in your counting and am overseeing the development of new plant life that will replace your world's reliance on animals as food. As Matthew has told you, flesh-eating will become unpalatable as people learn to respect the sanctity of animal life, and many will welcome other sources of protein with the same familiar flavors and consistency.

These plants will be introduced along with many other products and technologies when it is safe for your astral brotherhood to identify themselves and begin overtly assisting you to rapidly move forward in ways that will astonish you. That is, perhaps not so astonishing to you and other light-working souls, but to the masses of people who are living godly lives without understanding where the mammoth changes underway are leading. They see the old ways breaking down but don't know that when the phoenix rises from the ashes, so to say, a brilliant world awaits.

S: *It would be marvelous to meet you, Hugo—will you visit sometime?*

HUGO: Thank you, Madam Suzy, and yes, a visit later on is indeed a possibility, but not at this time as the density still there could entrap the body I would manifest. The many brothers now living among you took elaborate precautions prior to leaving their civilizations, and once on the planet, they underwent physical adaptation before emerging "full-fledged" into your society. But being there during this time is a mission they took on. As you know, my mission is considerably different, and I haven't the time for the adaptation process that would be necessary for even a brief visit.

S: Yes, I see, and your mission is a very important one! Thank you so much for visiting in spirit today, Hugo. I look forward to the time when we can meet.

HUGO: I, too, look forward to that day, which will be a time of rejoicing for all spiritual beings in this universe. And now, Madam Suzy, I take my leave and assure you that always I am at your service.

S: Thank you and goodbye for now, Hugo! Matthew?

MATTHEW: Good afternoon, Mother dear soul! Yes, I know of Hugo's visit. When you were pondering cloning, he and I talked, and even though I could answer your questions, we felt that you would greet his surprise visit with the joy you did.

S: Then thank you, too, Mash dear!

MATTHEW: Mother, let me take this opportunity to assure ALL peoples that any and every soul who is within their thoughts and feelings is only a breath away.

∾ 〇∾◎∾〇 ∾

REPTILIAN CIVILIZATION

S: What can you tell me about a "reptilian" civilization, Matthew?

MATTHEW: I know you've heard of this civilization as fearsome, Mother, but, simplistically speaking, some are good and some are not. The "good" ones can be trusted to be straightforward. I was most impressed with the two reptilians I met, who were spokesmen at a conference where preservation of the privacy of specific worlds was the primary issue. Invaders from another galaxy were entering ours, and those two leaders are powerful agents with forces that could prevent the spread of that invasion.

The reptilians are unlike other intellectually advanced civilizations in that they don't respect positions and hierarchies, they respect fighting power. Authorities not backed by armies and weaponry technology are not considered powerful in their view. They are intelligent beyond your imagining. Their brains are much larger than human brains and, from what I observed, they use them to the fullest capacity. Also, I have heard the same thing from sources more qualified than I to make that assessment. No one doubts their brilliance or their astute use of brain power in manifesting.

S: What do they look like?

MATTHEW: Those I met are shorter and slighter than the regular adult human, but not frail. Their skin is gray and they have no hair on their heads, but the

shape is attractive. Their eyes are black and piercing—
you can't look into their eyes and see into their souls.
I've been told that the form of the females is smoother
and rounder than the masculine form. That is the
appearance of this part of their population, but I can't
attest to that being the choice of any others. Since their
manifesting capability is so powerful, like other civilizations with that same level of capability, they can create
whatever forms they wish for housing their souls, and of
course they also can change their appearance whenever
they want.

They reproduce by mating, not by cloning. I suppose
they can clone, because it's a simple process, but they have
sexual reproductive systems and reproduce by those.
Again, this pertains to the group whose representatives I
met. We didn't get into a discussion of other reptilian
civilizations' lifestyle, appearance and activities, and no,
Mother, I have no idea how many reptilians there are in
total or where they all may reside.

I was able to talk with the two leaders in a small
group who met after the conference because my work with
transitioning souls was pertinent. It also is an important
aspect of their world. Their "afterlife" realm is not greatly
different from ours, but naturally it is in accordance with
their incarnate lives, intelligence, activities, life span—
just like us, with all the components of our physical life
being extended to our sanctuary realm. The leaders
seemed to be conscientious and diligent in a way we
would call humane and ethical.

*S: I'm trying to get an image of you talking with them.
I guess you're not sending me one. What did you wear
and what did they wear?*

MATTHEW: Fashion still isn't an interest we share, Mother. Let me recall. .... They wore simple, red shiny uniforms trimmed in black, with no medals or insignias. Probably I wore a business outfit more appropriate for that occasion than a white robe or jeans. Maybe I'm not sending you a picture because I can't remember what I wore.

S: Oh, right, Matthew! What about the "bad" reptilians?

MATTHEW: I haven't had personal contact with any, but I am well aware of the havoc they are causing on Earth and elsewhere in the universe. Those among you are not recognized as reptilian because of their assumed human forms, but they recognize each other. Indeed, they endeavor to keep their civilization pure by interbreeding, and they influence the human minds given to dark proclivity to assist in reaching their aims of total world domination. They are the embodiment of what you call evil, but more accurately stated, it is embodiment of the dense energy souls who are spiraling toward lost soul status.

Many reptilians are in combat with each other, as the "good" ones are as fiercely opposed to their "bad" counterparts creating such intense negativity as are any other light beings in physical form. Light is neither restricted to nor denied to any civilization or species—it is available to every soul of every civilization and species, and the dark forces will influence any willing soul of any nature anywhere.

PART VI

UNIVERSAL BROTHERHOOD

PROTHERO

MATTHEW: Mother, before Prothero starts his presentation I shall tell you something about this ancient soul who has a high degree of knowledge in harnessing energy for electrical use. His love for Earth is inherent in his core essence connection with the planet from its beginning, and his expertise in co-creating far exceeds most others who also were involved in those earliest stages. In his devotion to Earth, he volunteered a presentation for the book. Prothero is ready, Mother.

S: Prothero, I welcome you.

PROTHERO: Thank you and good day, Madam Suzanne. I welcome this meeting with you and this opportunity to be in God's service. I am a resident of this realm you call Heaven. As Matthew has told you, the name correctly is Nirvana. Most of my former lifetimes have been on Earth, but not exclusively. I also have lived in the placement called Sirius, whereby I came to know other cultures of human origin.

I shall begin the formal presentation. My topic is the accelerated learning being presented to Earth souls at this time. Opportunities for accelerated experiencing in mortal body now exist that never before have been presented on Earth. Your feelings and thoughts, not only your actions, are more crucial than ever before in these waning years prior to the closing of this millennium. "Cleansing" is a descriptive word of what will be happening as great changes occur on your planet.

This is not to frighten you! NEVER! It is to make you aware of this unique time in Earth history that is offering rapid completion of your selected lessons within the pre-birth agreement. It is essential that you complete all lessons during your lifetime or the entire lifetime must be repeated. Not only the missing parts must be repeated, but all events surrounding them, otherwise there can be no means for leading up to the missing experiences.

You may not clearly understand this prior to transitioning from your Earth lifetime to this realm. Such an understanding is not expected of you; however, that does not lessen the requirement for repeating an incomplete lifetime. The fact is, regardless of reason, less than complete mortal experiencing in accordance with your agreement is insufficient preparation for taking on a higher lifetime. For many souls, passage into this spirit realm is to prepare for another try at the identical conditions, personalities and genes that were not lived to their fullest intention in the immediate past physical lifetime.

This may seem unfair. It is more than fair when considered in the context of a soul being given another chance to fulfill the same set of lesson commitments even as other souls still are waiting for an opportunity to function in physical form.

Prior to this period in your planet's history, souls could spend hundreds or even many more lifetimes learning their chosen lessons, but now, time by your calendars is waning for mortal experiencing on Earth. There will be no more opportunities to fulfill your lifetime agreement or any other missing links in the pathways back to Oneness within the light of God. If this were not so, and if the cleansing were not vital and inevitable, there would not be this rushing to prepare souls for the coming times. Without spiritual integrity, the physical bodies cannot survive.

Here are guidelines for your preparation in awareness and wisdom to survive coming changes:

Do not be frightened! Fear is the opposite of love. You may think hatred is the opposite of love, but hatred is a by-product of fear. There is nothing to fear! A vital transition of planet Earth is in process, and fear is detrimental to your understanding and to your thinking positive, enlightening thoughts. Following your positive thoughts with positive actions is of utmost importance for fulfilling the mission you chose for your lifetime at hand.

When you chose your mission, you had all awareness of the times ahead and you eagerly arrived on Earth. However, after birth you forgot your chosen mission lessons except at soul level. Within your soul full knowledge of the lessons is clear and awaiting your conscious attunement.

Fright is deriving from dark forces operating within Earth's atmosphere. Beware of situations that cause you sinister feelings. Those feelings may be your soul advising you through intuition or conscience to avoid those situations, or maybe heavenly helpers are alerting you. Act wisely, in safety of your mortal and spiritual being. *Do not fear! Be aware!*

Do not shirk responsibilities intuitively known. These responsibilities are to family, to friends, to strangers and to yourself in accomplishing the plans your soul has in mind to follow. If you will meditate even for a short time to clear your mind of superfluous and disruptive thoughts, you will receive confidence in your proceedings. Your conscious connection is with God directly when you so listen and heed.

Allow the love of the Christed light to permeate your being. This is yours for only the asking. ASK! Open your thoughts as simply as "God, be with me," and God *is!*

Your help comes also from the heavenly helpers working in God's service and fulfilling their self-chosen missions. These are guardian angels, spirit guides and other beings from afar who have energy to spare and whose only purpose is to assist in the lifting of your own physical, emotional and mental energy. Again, please understand, *this help is yours for only the asking!*

Other avenues of reassurance, guidance and knowledge are throughout this book. If before this time of reading you were unaware of your connection with God and with all creations of God, and with your ever-present help therein, then let this book be your introduction to your guided pathway toward the light.

That concludes my presentation, Madam Suzanne. It is with greatest reverence for your work and service that I bid you good day and honor your assistance to all the world in this respect.

S: Thank you for that wise guidance, Prothero. And thank you also for your service. It is appropriate for me to say that, isn't it?

PROTHERO: Indeed so, Madam Suzanne! I shall add, I believe my presentation is not without flaws in form and expression. It is my understanding and concurrence that your hand in fine tuning words without distortion of meaning is to be used throughout the material for this book. I ask that you provide my presentation with the same agility as you shall be doing for the other presenters.

And now, I shall take my leave of this moment of communion with you. In love and shining radiance, I am your servant, Prothero.

S: Goodbye, Prothero, and again, thank you. Matthew, are you here?

MATTHEW: Yes, Mother, and I know you are wondering how Prothero's presentation can be salvaged from its scrambled form. He was able to discern this easily, and that's why he asked for your "fine tuning." Because of his love for Earth from antiquity forward, Prothero wanted to give you a message for her people. None of his lifetimes on the planet were in English-speaking nations and most of them were long before that language even existed, so he quickly studied English because he wished to speak personally with you rather than use the universal translation mode.

Wording and organization of his presentation is "flawed," as he says, but the content is most significant. So please do work with it. As always, you will be guided in the changes. Never fear, you will not be imposing your own thoughts upon his message!

Prothero spoke hesitantly and quietly at the beginning of his transmission and gained confidence as he proceeded. Although considerable reorganization and other editing were needed to make his message more comprehensible than his exact words in the order he gave them, much of his phraseology and all of his fervor are preserved.

MENTA

MENTA: Good morning, Ms. Suzy! I am here in the brotherhood of all humankind. We are your friends! The important message I bring to you is in alignment with the energies being beamed across the universe to heal your planet. Without this help, Earth would not recover from the insufficient oxygen in her atmosphere or the negative vibrations and chemical pollutants that are the result of the collective thoughts, actions and sensations of her humankind.

Behind this oxygen deprivation that causes a veil over your consciousness, negativity and pollution is the heavy influence of the dark forces at work most diligently and incessantly. There are within those forces true sparks of Creator, the Supreme Being over all the universes in the cosmos, as everything in existence comes from Creator's energy except darkness itself. Darkness could not come from Creator, whose essence is pure love-light. Everything throughout the cosmos in form or without form, or as you say, "discarnate," starts with an idea, and the highest, purest beings came from Creator's idea to express Itself into those very first souls you call archangels.

Only love-light existed in that realm of perfection for an unknown passage of time in Deepest Ages. At some point the highest of the angels asked Creator to let them use Its energy so they could express their own ideas into existence. Creator gave them what you call the "gift of free will," which let them CO-create with Creator.

In the Beginning all of the angels' ideas were in line with Creator's and together they made the lower angels and gods and goddesses. All of those souls were made of the same love-light energy as Creator. But eventually some angels had ideas to make horrible, miserable creatures and found much enjoyment in doing so. Never was such a thing Creator's intention!

But even when those angels made still worse creatures and lost their angel status by moving so far away from the light of Source, Creator kept Its promise about their free will. They and their foul ideas, which are indestructible substances called thought forms, became the gigantic energy field known as "the dark forces." Yet always the soul sparks within those forces have been connected to Creator because Its energy is their very life force. Each universe is a microcosm of the cosmos, so ever since darkness began those untold eons past, all souls throughout all universes have had the free will to use Creator's infinite energy for either light or dark, according to their ideas.

Creator picked some of the gods and goddesses to be the rulers of the universes and co-create everything in them, and in this way you are inseparably connected with Creator through the reigning god of this universe. The only law Creator gave to those rulers is that always they must honor Its free will gift to all souls in their particular domain. Therefore, you have the right to choose what to co-create with this god that you call by God and other names. Ms. Suzy, with respect to your customary name for this highest power in this universe, I will say God. Using God's energy, each of you choose and create your life situations by your own ideas, your thoughts that are of light essence or of the dark, and in that same way all of you together make everything that is in your world.

You see, there is no difference in the process that

produced the highest angels from the process of planting a flower seed and seeing its life force grow into a blossom. It is the same with allowing a talent to develop and flourish. Those spring from ideas, from the thoughts of various souls taking form, and from other ideas come beings in all other forms: animals and plants of every kind; mountains and lakes; all objects; paintings and music; volcanoes and quakes and other forces of nature. Everything in your world is the product of some idea, and not all are of beauty or goodness.

Some ideas produce sickness, pollution, wars and greediness, and the revelation will come forth as to what this kind of co-creation means for all humankind and for dear Earth herself. You have become mired too deeply in third density to hear and see and think beyond this low level sensing. That is a pity, because only a breath away there is a wondrous universe for you to explore, but the glories awaiting your discovery cannot exist within a *perception* that is narrow and confined in its vision and sensing. However, the higher energies now swirling around your planet offer a great opportunity to change that narrowness in outlook.

We know from our success with this meditation exercise I shall explain that it can help you open your minds and align you with the higher frequencies wherein you can experience the wonders surrounding and within you. So, let nothing distract you as you begin the exercise with a short prayer. This can be *"God of light and love, please grant me now the awakening of my consciousness into your other worlds"* or similar words more comfortable for you.

1. Lie on your back and fold your arms across your chest, palms down, and close your eyes, but do not go to

sleep. Allow your thoughts to drift and swirl as they please until they waft away.

2. With your inner eye, focus on the image of a bright blue sky, which may have clouds for the reality of your sky. Let your mind relax in this image until you feel tranquil. If thoughts come into your picture, gently ask them to leave.

3. When you feel completely tranquil, see an image of yourself in the sky—remembering a photo likeness is the easiest way to achieve this.

4. Focus on your image until it seems to be moving serenely—actually, it is moving with the energy. Thereafter the image will take off into its own choice of sphere or contact.

5. Allow other images and messages to float into your mind, but insofar as possible, do not react to them. Record any messages after completing this meditation exercise.

It may take a few days for this exercise to produce messages, and those may be brief, coming as strange sounds or images in an unfamiliar context. The messages may seem unrelated to anything you have experienced or imagined, but they are significant. This is a period of breaking through the "veil" of third density and remembering what you already do know at soul level but have forgotten consciously. Longer periods of hearing, sensing and visioning will follow.

Very well, Ms. Suzy, thank you. That is enough message for this day. I know you have questions in your mind about my people and more. Would you like me to answer those now?

S: *Yes please, Menta.*

MENTA: Then I begin. We are a vast and powerful
energy field of a billion or so collective souls. When we
embody, we live on a planet called Retorno in a galaxy
beyond the constellation Lyra. Our homeland is one of
many inhabited worlds not yet seen by your telescopes.
I shall explain why I say "I" and "we" interchangeably. It
is because I speak with you as a soul self, but never am
I separate from our group mind. No soul is considered
better than another as all aspects of our mind are
necessary for our world's stability and our ever-growing
awareness.

We are not as balanced in some ways as others. That
is why we think of ourselves as "feminine" because with
those thoughts, we draw to us the gentle strength,
patience, nurturing, peacefulness, artistry through
imagination, and the wisdom of heeding intuition that
are associated with goddess energy.

As collective selves we resemble a tree much more
than a human because our "head" area is an abundance
of sensors that look like flowers in a tight cluster. That
is the "housing unit" of the group mind. White is the
predominant color of this head area, but pastel colors
also are seen—they are the colors of specialty areas such
as the arts, technology, engineering, child rearing and so
forth. We are an array of the colors most closely identified
with the primary talents and abilities and interests at a
particular time, so the colors change to reflect the
frequency in which we are operating. That is, it's the
facet of the prism refracted into the color identified with
that frequency.

Connected to the "housing unit" cluster and extending
throughout galaxies are a billion or more fine "threads."
Those are our soul selves roaming the heavens in search
of new knowledge, or more accurately, *remembering*,

because at highest soul awareness level everything is known. All soul-self discoveries instantaneously and automatically are transmitted to the group mind.

Ms. Suzy, I shall send you an image.

S: Thank you, Menta. I'm seeing a gigantic network of twinkling lights moving about like shooting stars.

MENTA: You are seeing a good likeness, but within the minute scope of the mind's eye it is impossible to detect our vastness. Although we can move freely throughout the heavens forever twinkling, your telescopes will never see us because we are flickering lights rather than sustained light.

S: I see. Menta, since you can embody as individual souls, are any of you in human form here?

MENTA: We could do that and look no different from you, but we have no reason to do so at this time because our assistance to you does not require us to be on the planet like the many "extraterrestrials" who are living among you. I don't wish to offend, Ms. Suzy, but we see as huge beautiful lights those highly evolved souls who left their homelands to "walk in" by agreement or who were born into human bodies specifically to serve Earth's needs in this critical time, and the few you do see are regarded as merely entertainment spectacles. I don't wish to speak more about those individuals except to say that you are mentally identifying them correctly.

S: I understand, Menta. May I ask you another question?

MENTA: I am at your service in total, Ms. Suzy. Please ask.

S: What is your interest in helping us and in giving me information for this book?

MENTA: They are one and the same! We are magically endowed with suprahuman eyes of dimensions for seeing all happenings and therefore see the forthcoming changes on Earth. Those are her natural defenses to rid her planetary body of the negativity that threatens its survival. During the period of correcting those conditions, you will need the friendship of other civilizations that most of you cannot even imagine exist.

We are more powerful than many others who also are helping to their full intensity, but their wavelength is less than ours, so we volunteered for a twofold mission. We are beaming in our own energy and also sustaining the light from those other sources once it is within Earth's atmosphere. This is essential so that your bodies can absorb the rays at cellular level and adjust to the higher frequencies Earth will be entering. This gives you the opportunity to physically survive during her ascension process that some call "the shift" and others call "the cleansing."

S: Menta, thank you for caring about us! Who asked you to help us?

MENTA: A cry for help from Earth herself reached throughout the heavens, and out of concern for this once beautiful planet whose soul always has been pure and radiant, we responded.

S: Can you describe the sound of Earth's cry?

MENTA: It was a weary sound of resignation, like a faint echo of a once healthy life that had become too feeble to call out loudly. That weak sound signified that Earth was near death due to her environmental conditions, and we wanted to help her survive and be restored to health. God authorizes a genuinely unselfish response to such a request for help, but no intervention is permitted except by invitation to participate jointly in the venture.

Our governing body approached the Intergalactic Council high authority and volunteered our services. Understanding Earth's condition and her "cry of invitation," the Council sanctioned our participation after being assured that our interest was not self-serving. That is, we would give all necessary assistance solely for the good of Earth and not take advantage of her weakened condition to conquer her peoples. Not only would we never think of such an act of betrayal, but an indication of conquest intent would mean a declaration of war with peacekeepers of the cosmos, and *NEVER* would we choose that condition! War is not a province of feminine energy, only of masculine, and we have absolutely no interest in it.

And now, Ms. Suzy, perhaps that is enough for today. I thank you for your graciousness in receiving from us and for this opportunity extended to us to contribute to this information service for Earth.

S: Thank you for today, Menta. I look forward to being with you tomorrow. Matthew?

MATTHEW: Mother, I am here, and I know you feel that was a dream. Menta is an entity of such magnitude and vastness that your sensation within her energy is quite different from that within your other sources. It was a sublime experience for me to observe that communication from my vantage point of seeing this unique energy in its twinkling effect, its full scope of grandeur. It was spectacular! I'm glad you were able to achieve the vision for yourself, even though from your vantage point it is all confined to a small screen within your mind. From here, I see as if through a gigantic window. You're wondering if she sent you a hologram— yes, an image of the Menta force moving about the heavens.

The following day:

MENTA: One day all souls in the universe once again will be reunited consciously and reintegrate with God, but that is far ahead because many deceivers and betrayers are not yet spiritually aware that this is the ultimate goal of all beings. At this moment they have no interest in remembering, only in their plundering and creating havoc in the heavens.

Yesterday I spoke about the darkness that evokes that kind of behavior. Darkness is a potential that exists within each soul side by side with light, like two sides of a coin, and just as in a real coin where there is no division, always there is the choice which side to have "up." When you keep your "up-side" in the light and absorb its essence, it is your choice to develop the potential for god-ness, for growing within the influence of God light. Both "light" and "dark" sides of a coin have value, do they not? So, when the "down" dark side becomes the "up" dark side, it has as much potential as the light side that no longer is exposed.

That is a simplistic example of the inseparability of the potentials for "good" and "bad" within each person, but it suffices for you to easily imagine and apply to your life choices. You have control of self to the same extent that you have over which side of the coin to expose to view. Both sides and their potentials cannot be exposed simultaneously, and neither can your soul perform within light and within darkness at the same time. Always it is a choice as to which potential force you will permit to be active.

Just as the rim of the coin bands both sides, conscience is the band of both the light and the dark potentials within you, but it is designed to be your guide in choosing an action or an attitude *within the light potential.* When you feel a "pinching" at some thought or decision, your conscience is nimbly alerting you that the choice is not "good." Linkage is possible with either the light or the darkness, and knowing which potential to choose is as simple as letting your conscience be a guiding light to your footsteps in soul growth!

If conscience is ignored time after time, its elasticity is lost and it becomes hardened, unable to alert about a "bad" choice, and thus conscience is lost for all intent of its purpose. You say, *"That person 'has no conscience,' "* and you are correct insofar as the effectiveness of conscience, which is no more—it was taken over by the potential for darkness.

However, it must be understood that choices are neither good nor bad except by *judgment.* You may say that free will allows all choices, and that is correct, but there is a pit full of choice options within the light and dark potentials, and it is the collective choices of the life-time that are one's energy record of service unto self—that is, according to selections made before birth—or unto the dark forces. Choose wisely, as time is shortening, and at the day of reckoning, there can be no erasing of choices in the dark just as there can be no adding to choices in the light.

You have a question, Ms. Suzy.

S: Menta, I was wondering if conscience works the same way in a group mind—is there a collective conscience?

MENTA: The ONLY way a group mind could be negotiated is by the inclusion of conscience! An inherent part of all life forms with intelligence above rock and sand is instinctiveness, and the higher the intelligence factor, the greater the scope of conscience. In group mind there is magnified conscience, which enables all souls within the mind to know instinctively the choices within the light and those within the darkness.

It is our mission by choice to follow the light. In this pathway is our opportunity to be of service to you in your coming time of enormous changes. We are your friends, and now we shall return to the home base and continue serving the needs of Earth in her restoration to beauty and health. Adieu and salu.

S: Good day to you, Menta. Welcome back.

MENTA: Indeed a good day, Ms. Suzy! I am happy to return and give more information for your use in a book.

Disintegration of the inherited pure love-light energy of Creator took place rapidly after souls' first taste of exercising the free will gift to manifest with Creator energy. When it became known throughout the cosmos that integrity was lacking in some early beings' energy streams, it became instantly apparent that further disintegration would happen without some form of curtailment.

What had happened is that the energy component that you may call Satan, Lucifer, the devil, Beelzebub or other names, strayed from its inheritance essence and allowed currents of greed and deceit to enter its awareness. From whence came those currents? From the BEGINNING! All that you call negative and all you call positive derived in the same moment, the first splitting of Creator essence, and from that have come permutations of undesirable and unanticipated energy forces with negatively charged currents.

However, once it was discovered that the balancing of ALL energy was required, as negative "bad" became worse, positive "good" became better. There are absolutes in "down" and "up" on the balancing scale, and for Earth to meet her balancing schedule, she needed help to attract positive energy components to bring her divinity and health into order once more.

You speak of "the righteous inheriting the Earth," but no "righteous" want Earth in her current condition! Therefore, the inheritors are asking for assistance in their reclamation of a peaceful, healthful and beauteous Earth. Harmony of human mind and planetary consciousness through reunification and love is the path we are now on with each soul on Earth who is so willing.

You would be in awe if you were able to perceive with eyes and ears the sights and sounds of Earth in travail and the "physician" assistance coming to heed these cries! There is sorrow to diminish and turn back into joy, as it is the energy of joy that is the balance needed to sustain the life of soil and water and human selves. All is ready for the intricate dance to begin to bring the teeter-totter of opposing energy attachments into a sustainable balance.

Then there will be the fulcrum for the swaying and righting motion, and also for sustaining the hearts and minds of Earth souls in their cellular balance that is needed for meeting the space brotherhood on equal grounds. Then there will be the alignment of Earth's consciousness with her inhabitants' consciousness, which is necessary for the evolution of the wholeness of all on Earth because that wholeness leads to reintegration with God. Do you see, Ms. Suzy?

S: Menta, it is a great deal to see. It is beyond my conscious comprehension.

MENTA: Ah, but not on the other level of your comprehension that supersedes your conscious thought and functioning! Your supraconscious state, when all of your consciousness is totally focused on the lighted path, HAS this knowledge! Your narrow silver cord, as you think of your attachment to the universe, is no different from our attachments except in the scope of attunement with the universal rhythm—not in the scope of your awareness, but only of your individual amount of alignment. It is like this: An apple is its same essence and importance whether on a table alone or in an orchard with many thousands of other apples of equal quality and importance.

S: Thank you for that extra explanation, Menta. Do you know anything about prior civilizations here, such as Atlanteans or Lemurians?

MENTA: Yes, I am aware of their existence and their influence in individual souls living on Earth today. That isn't hidden information, Ms. Suzy.

S: It seems to be hidden from most of us here. Does your assistance to us include meeting with any government leaders or other influential people here?

MENTA: That is not our method of assistance in this planetary transition, and we do not wish to interact with government leaders. Those of the brotherhood who have done so have not been pleased with their reception or subsequent developments, including the deliberate killing of some of these benevolent beings, and it is not our interest to pursue this type of discourse.

S: Do you have spirit guides or a guardian angel?

MENTA: We don't know whether spirit guides would be useful to us, but we have none of those, and neither do we have a guardian angel. We understand the concept of such beings and think it delightful, but our group self has no need for a separate being to float above us and touch down in moments to see if everything is all right with us. Do you see?

S: Well, I see that you are satisfied with yourselves insofar as protection, enlightenment and your spiritual path. You may have your angel within your group mind.

MENTA: That is an interesting thought! That is far more original thinking than you are surmising. Most noteworthy, Ms. Suzy. We shall not reply further on this, please.

S: That's fine, Menta. I believe this is the last time we'll be speaking. Is there anything else you would like to say?

MENTA: Thank you, Ms. Suzy. I say it is the pleasure of this Menta force to have this opportunity to greet all of you souls in Earth bodies and encourage you to look inward and upward. Within your soul's knowing but not your conscious remembering, is the Beginnings when all was understood, wherein lies the key to conscious unity once again within the universal community.

After sleeping time, allow the memory of your rediscovered self to remain. Keep the potential for goodness as the "up-side" to right your balance and sustain it. Know the importance of belief, and believe that you are important, but not exclusive in God's love. Believe that others we have called your brothers, but who do not look like your family, are serving to stabilize your home planet so she can achieve balance and the same with all of you receptive ones.

My people—different from you in appearance but of corresponding grace within—give you our assurance that our assistance will continue in peacefulness throughout the period of reformation in your world. Now, in fellowship and brotherhood, I leave our message within these pages for your contemplation and accept-ance in the same loving spirit that we continue to serve Earth in her restoration to health and beauty. Salu.

S: Goodbye, Menta. Thank you for your messages. Thank you for your interest in us and for your help.

MATTHEW: Mother, Menta's energy has left.

S: She didn't hear me thank her?

MATTHEW: Always appreciation of genuine nature is reached between two energies. She is fully aware of your feelings as they were in a lighted stance throughout the transmission. It has been most interesting for me to observe these transmissions. Only when others are communicating with you can I see how your welcome and gratitude are in a parallel lighted stream with your doubting and questioning. When you feel comfortable with the information, this dual flow merges, and when you have even a little doubt, a slender ribbon of energy flows alongside the major one of acceptance, appreciation and wonderment.

2008:

To accommodate new material for this revision, Menta worked with me to reduce her message to about half its original length, but without sacrificing anything she feels is vital for you to know. For translators' benefit, she also simplified her speaking style, but some of its unusual "flavor" remains.

She told me that during the fourteen years between her original message and this edited version, her people have observed the powerful effects of the light that they and other civilizations have been constantly beaming to Earth: Earth's strengthened planetary body has been ascending on a steady course toward fourth density, and light-receptive individuals' cellular structure is changing from carbon to crystalline so they can physically accompany Earth on her journey. At the conclusion of our editing process, Menta said, "Ms. Suzy, we are friends from so far back that you have no idea, but someday you will. All of Earth's peoples then will know their rightful place in our universal family."

LAZARUS

[Lazarus pronounces his name with the accent on the first syllable.]

MATTHEW: Mother, the next presentation is from a soul representing the Lazarus energy, which is highly respected universally. This massive force was assigned by God to reduce the destructive effects of the negativity that has so polluted Earth that it almost killed her planetary body. Lazarus is ready to begin his presentation.

LAZARUS: Good morning, Mistress Suzy. We are a group of souls who are more powerful than many fine souls who simply have had far fewer lifetimes to evolve than we.

Although the planetary cleansing cannot be avoided, the amount of destruction can be lessened by reducing the bombardment of negativity and the scope of its effects. Performing this service is an assignment that we undertake with enthusiasm! Our message is to explain what caused the negativity, why it must be eliminated, and to help you prepare spiritually for the changes the cleansing will bring.

The god that Creator selected to rule this universe is called by God and other names, but we shall call Him God with respect to your familiarity with that name, Mistress Suzy. There are enemies of God that are violent, and although less powerful than God, they are formidable indeed. God is light and the enemies are the opposite, so they can be appropriately called the "dark forces." The forces' energy that is prevalent in your world caused the negativity that has dulled souls' consciousness and prevented their evolution toward the light.

The enormity of the cleansing required to eliminate the negativity is considerable in this unprecedented time in Earth's history, and spiritual preparation for this process requires forthcoming revelations that may be shocking. If fear is your first reaction, do not think it is your fault. The dark forces are ever near to instill fear of God within you—NEVER is there a reason to fear God! You need not fear the dark forces either, as the Christed light within your soul can shatter their effects and illuminate your pathway. That light is your connection to the Almighty Oneness that never was broken, only forgotten by you.

Energy is totally neutral, but by dark design, negatively-charged energy, more simply called negativity, is violent and destructive. Energy is indestructible, so the only way to dissipate negativity, which stores itself in such tight mass that it can kill a planet, is to dislodge it and transmute it into light. Doing so is what the cleansing, or "the shift," is all about.

The negativity polluting Earth has come from millennia of her inhabitants' fear, greed, brutality and rambunctious sexual behaviors, corruption in your leaders, deceit from your churches, foul education of young minds. This, dear ones, is pollution of the most vicious nature! Earth is a sentient being, a loving soul, and she was in despair because her planet body was dying from the negativity that was created by the energy charges of those vicious thoughts, intentions and deeds. God, in His infinite love and wisdom and power, decreed that Earth shall NOT be killed as other planets and their civilizations have been. The salvation of Earth and

YOU is the reason for the cleansing! It will raise the consciousness of souls on the planet and uplift Earth's soul from despair and restore her body to its original health, purity and beauty.

You think of "natural disasters" as not affecting you if they are far away, but each jolt of Earth's crust and interior creates changes in your psyche and every cell of your body. These connections are by the universal laws that you agreed upon in antiquity. How so? Some of you believe in reincarnation, others scoff at it. Well, scoffing does not change the fact of multiple lifetimes in physical forms, some different from human, that all souls need for returning to their Beginnings in the Almighty Oneness.

We are not the only ones eager to help you and your Mother Earth continue on her ascension journey. Others in flagships and mother ships have been present in your atmosphere for well over half a century of your years. While some of these beings are merely curious about the drama unfolding in this solar system, most are friends who have come to your rescue! Like we, they come only with love and peaceful intent to assist you and Earth!

Their lives are as important to them as yours are to you. Yet, when these friends—your universal family!—landed to bring messages of great importance for your individual and planetary survival, they have been killed or captured and imprisoned to die. Why? To keep you ignorant of their very existence and ignorant of truths they would reveal that the dark forces want to keep hidden from you.

Through the influence of the dark forces, the ones among you who are responsible for hiding the truths also have the intention to enslave your body, mind and soul. Your governments have been betraying you and your religions have been so infiltrated that the true message given by God's major messenger, Jesus the Christ, has been deliberately distorted by the story of the cross and resurrection. The message that Jesus brought directly from God was that *you are part of God*—NEVER separate, only individual in a body for living and learning.

Jesus was not meant to die on a cross, and in fact, he did not. That false story about his death and resurrection was devised to make Jesus the "only son of God," but he was the son of God no more and no less than you! The great difference is, Jesus knew his direct, inseparable connection with God and he used that connection to perform what you call "miracles." EVERY soul is a child of God and has the inherent ability to co-create with Him! Souls throughout this universe never are separate from Him or from one another, and this connection exists throughout your animal and plant kingdoms just as it does in all other civilizations. It is not a sacrilege to recognize and proclaim, *"I am God."* Your soul essence is the same as God's, but His magnitude and power is beyond your comprehension.

The truth about "church" has been distorted too. Buildings are not church, dogmas are not church. Church is the communion between each soul and God directly, without layers of supplicants to pass on prayers. Prayers are your every thought and feeling, and all are known to God. Your every wish, your every intention, your every act of mercy or foolishness—or so in your eyes—is known to God.

Mistress Suzy, we have the Council's permission to continue our presentation another day. We know the questions in your mind about our appearance and civilization and so forth, but beings with equal interest in helping you and your planet have come to give you their message and we don't wish to delay them. Icarus is the name of this group—yes, like the mythical flyer with waxed wings, but from eons prior to that story. Now we take our leave so Icarus can speak.

ICARUS

ICARUS: Good day, Mistress Suzy. Thank you for accommodating us with such speed and willingness. We were notified late about the cleansing and preservation project and arrived from our homeland Redondole, near Sirius, later than many others who also came to help Earth-Gaia-Terra-Shan. *[Redondole is pronounced ray-don'-doe-lay.]*

It is our pleasure and pride to be involved. This project is of foreign nature to us as we have been confined for all time to other constellations, where growth is in goodness and truth. God has allowed us this privilege to assist in lessening the trauma of planetary changes and uplifting the consciousness of your civilization. We are eager to place our troops at your disposal!

You have mentally questioned the appearance and specific involvement of the Lazarus energy, so we are assuming that you would like the same information from us.

S: Yes, Icarus, I would, but please continue as you wish.

ICARUS: Very well, thank you. Icarus, like many other names in your mythology, descended from fact. The mythological Icarus is so named because of his golden wings of wax, a symbolic inspiration that came from our space fleet. We are in possession of a fine fleet due to far-advanced intelligence and superior technology that derive from our fuller brain usage than your current civilization. This is not spoken egotistically, Mistress

Suzy, only factually. Our power for fuel, heat, lighting—
all needs—comes directly from sources provided by God.

We are sending you our image. As you see, we are not
humanoid in appearance, but only in our natural habitat
do we appear tall, rangy, silver and very, very thin, with
large eyes and long nimble fingers. We do not much care
for the "spider" of your thought, but it is your comparison
and so we accept it.

We can embody to look exactly like any form we
imagine or wish to imitate, including just like you. That
is how many of us are among you already and you are
not the least bit aware of it! We are assisting in the
cleansing by being in influential positions so we can
make a difference in decisions that affect the environment, the pollution and industries, and in other ways
that can reduce the negativity on Earth and therefore
reduce the destruction of terra firma and seas.

We are part of a force in Earth human disguise that
cannot openly declare its presence or purpose, which is
the very salvation of your planet! We would like to be
known as who we are naturally and no longer hide
among you. However, it is not yet time according to our
messages directly from God, who rules all major
decisions in this universe and has His own timetable for
optimum benefits to all concerned.

We are eager in all respects to assist and not take
over any aspect of your self-governing that is according
to the laws of God and the universe. We will honor all self-
rule and decisions unless these are aimed —as so many
are—at self-destruction and planetary destruction. Then
we are empowered to technologically oppose those
forces, to prevent what would be so traumatically
destructive to the planet and lives.

I shall explain. Creator's free will gift got out of hand

long ago. Nevertheless, that gift has been honored continuously without intervention until this time. Acting on Creator's mandate, the highest cosmic councils declared that there would be no more nuclear or atomic explosions in space, which have damaged souls even at such a distance from the explosion that you cannot imagine it. I speak not of temporal bodies, but of souls, which are eternal parts of God. Therefore, that one exception was made to honoring free will, and we would be part of the energy force that would prevent such a destructive attempt.

We do not wish to outstay our welcome or say more than is necessary. We are willing to return to answer questions if you wish, but we feel that our statement is enough and more would be superfluous. Do you wish to add anything?

S: Thank you for coming today, Icarus. I am curious why you came "through" me. And will you return to talk about your home, your history and your future among us?

ICARUS: We are more than happy to be here at God's invitation to contribute to your book and would be most happy to return at any time you invite us. We are on an invitational basis, as are all beings of light, so as not to invade the privacy guaranteed by universal laws. If you extend the invitation, we will return and discuss the information you mentioned and perhaps more of our own that you may not think to ask.

Now, with grace and love we take our leave. One day we shall greet you warmly in the streets of your cities and perhaps much sooner in your dream state. Good day and goodbye for the moment.

2008:

I didn't invite Icarus to return after he gave me his presentation in 1994—organizing, indexing and editing the many transmissions became so ponderous that I forgot about his gracious offer. However, when I was reviewing his message for final manuscript preparation and, many years later, during the revision process (none of his original presentation was changed), Icarus greeted me in high spirits and encouragement about Earth's ascension progress. He said the members of his civilization living among us are fulfilling their assistance assignments and eagerly looking forward to the joyous day when they can introduce themselves.

LAZARUS

S: Good morning and welcome back, Lazarus.

LAZARUS: Mistress Suzy, we greet you as well, but for us, it is not "back" because our energy never left you. We shall continue our presentation and then will be pleased to answer your questions.

Along with the light in each soul are other forces far beyond your imagining, but that you must reckon with. These are the dark forces we spoke about before. You must look within yourself and determine if you have allowed their influence to govern the life choices you have made.

How can you distinguish the darkness from the light? Ask "the energy" stirring within you—that which defines your interests and desires and motivates you to act as you do—if it is from the light. According to the laws of the universe, truth must be told or evidence of the lie must be shown. Expect no truth from the dark forces—truth is not their way—but they cannot hide their presence.

Relax, close your eyes and tell the energy within you to show itself. Still your mind and let images and colors come. If you see brilliant white and gold, with perhaps tinges of pastel colors, and this light can be sustained, you can be confident that you are aligned with the forces of God that gave you self-empowerment. Sustained golden white light is the Christed light and identifies the light forces. Purple, or violet, rays also are of the light.

Mingled dark colors, particularly flames of red with

darkness behind them, reveal that darkness is the source of your ideas, intentions and actions. Even if you may sense that you are hearing *"We are light,"* tongues of flame are evidence of the dark forces' presence. You have given over to them your God-given powers.

If this exercise produced that flame kind of dark image, DEMAND that only light may enter you! Ask for the help of the divine forces of Christed light to rid you of the poisonous darkness. Ask and ye shall receive—it is that easy!

We are a group of souls as huge as your galaxy and with corresponding powers, yet we are speaking in terms we understand and you understand. It is the same truth brought by messengers from God in previous centuries, the truth of your godself.

Mistress Suzy, thank you for recording our presentation, and now we would like to answer your questions to your satisfaction.

S: Thank you, Lazarus, for your extremely informative presentation. Why were you chosen to give it?

LAZARUS: Because of our capability and willingness to assist Earth in relieving the negativity, the Council asked us to give you information about that for the book. We are in spirit brothers, we and you, and therefore natural collaborators in God's service. We are among the millions of your universal family whose crafts have been surrounding your planet on "active duty" for fifty years or more, relieving Earth of the negativity that nearly killed her planetary body.

S: How do you relieve negativity?

LAZARUS: We combine our energy with other entities who also want to preserve Earth's life. We came en masse to breathe our energy into her lungs, which are the air, the atmosphere, to withdraw many of the pollutants that were killing her.

We are not warriors, we are more engineering minds. Our energy has been helping to stabilize the planet and hold steady its orbit through areas where other heavenly bodies could seriously affect orbiting stability. We harness, or level out, the effects of what you call "natural disasters" to prevent the widespread destruction that otherwise would occur. We withdraw force from the energy fomenting beneath the surface that would produce volcanic eruptions of such magnitude they would blow up entire mountains and destroy surrounding towns. We stabilize fault lines so earthquakes are less severe—they still release energy, but do not destroy the vast areas they could without our softening interference.

We quiet the seas and temper the wind forces so you don't have the extent of hurricanes, cyclones and tornadoes and flooded coastal areas that you would if we did not do this. We alter the course of celestial fragments within impact distance of Earth. We keep a rhythm going that is required of all your life forces.

Are these examples clear as to our cleansing participation?

S: Yes, and all of this is amazing! Thank you for these great services to Earth, Lazarus. Please tell me about yourself, or selves, and your homeland and history. What do you look like? Are any of you living on Earth?

LAZARUS: You stun us! You would want to know about ourselves? This would be of interest to people on Earth?

*S: YES! Please tell us everything that will enlighten
us about you.*

LAZARUS: Well then, I shall continue. To describe
the appearance of our group entity, energetically that is,
imagine the effects of a high wind through tall
evergreens, a strong sweeping motion at the top and a
strong whirring sound, and along the ground, gentler
movement and sounds. That is a good way to imagine us.
There is no face, no form, no color, only sound and
motion in our energy that covers an area larger than
your solar system.

We wanted to evolve as collective souls but were
limited by the low intellectual capacity of some
members. "Group entity" or "group mind" means that all
members may share the energy generated by the finest,
but diluted by the weakest. Rather than exclude the
intellectually weaker souls within our group, we elected
to merge our individual consciousness into a major force
with unity of purpose and direction.We have not regretted
this decision and have learned that we can individuate,
live as individual souls, and still retain the group soul
focus toward the light. Our incarnation began in
Sirius—many habitable planets in that constellation are
comparable to Earth in all essential life-sustaining
ways—and we became a very small percentage of the
Sirian civilization. Our group energy that wished to
experience in embodied form did so by contact of physical
bodies for conception and birthing.

Our whole energy never was nor is now incarnate,
but the streamers that do embody resemble your white
races in form and features, and in tenacity and mind
power we resemble your red races. While physical
stature is important because it determines activities of

physical strength and interest, it is *soul identification*
that is the absolute, and here we bow to our kindred
spirits, your indigenous peoples. Also we have lent energy
particles to some souls who wished to experience in
other civilizations or as animals. Many whales on Earth
in past eras had our energy, but because of the slaughter
that began some two hundred years or more back in your
history, all of that has returned to our group energy and
continues to serve Earth within our "greatest" self.

To return to our history, as our small homeland planet
began to stray from orbit, perhaps three to four million
of your years back, we realized through our soul connection
with God that our physical lives would be lost if we did
not prepare to avert potential planetary destruction. We
decided to synthesize all intellectual and spiritual
knowledge and energize our minds into a single purpose.
That focus enabled us to stabilize our planet's orbit and
save the physical bodies of our people, who numbered
over five billion in energy calculation of collective souls.
We retained the music that had been inspired for our
people directly from the angels—that music is one of the
most essential aspects of our energy focus.

Our home in part is the one in Sirius, but over time
we learned that Earth offered a new beginning free of
intellectual pollution, a status not yet achieved in your
linear time but already manifested in the continuum, so
we are living among you *in spirit only.* Do not ever fear
that our presence is as captor to you as our captive!
NEVER! *We were led here directly by God to work in
energy only.*

S: *In what ways are you using your energy here?*

LAZARUS: The ways you can identify with are in

nature, physics, the power of combined natural elements. We are making our course toward the light more direct, without the deviations of war and conflict of issues, which is why God directed us to Earth. If only you people could see from our vantage point the energy you are wasting in your bickering and wars, you would instantly stop!

S: Lazarus, most of us want that to stop! Are you in the collective energy or have you taken on a body?

LAZARUS: I am smiling at your question, Mistress Suzy! In this moment I am with you in energy only, but during these times of such enormous changes in the universe, usually I am in one form or another, depending on my service and location. For some time I have been aboard the mother ship hovering nearby Earth, but when situations are quiet, in a fleeting second I can be at home with my dear family in Sirius.

S: Oh! Will you and the others in spacecrafts land so we can meet you?

LAZARUS: Oh yes, but not until there is assurance of safety for us and all who would be at the landing sites. Many of you believe that we come in peace and *your governments know this!* They know that when we publicly appear, it means the end of their greed, deceit and control, so they would not be pleased to see us.

S: I understand. What do your spacecraft look like? Please tell us about sites and anything else pertaining to landings. Can any of us travel with you?

LAZARUS: We have several types of crafts. There are small reconnaissance ships that comfortably hold eight persons, and the largest in your vicinity is our mother ship, which can hold New York City in geographic size and population.

We are part of the mammoth intergalactic fleet operating within the highest Council's landing plans and coordination. At this point general areas for our small crafts have been chosen, but no specific spots. Signals prior to landing will be soft tones and lights to indicate there's nothing to fear. The crafts will be made very obvious prior to landing so people may come to greet us if they want to. Telepathy is our common form of communication, but we speak your languages—yes, we studied them, Mistress Suzy—so there will be no problem at all with communication.

Speaking for the Lazarus group, for the first landing I think about a hundred of our small craft will land simultaneously in outlying areas all over the planet, away from areas where there could be immediate response from military or other belligerent forces. There will be both male and female adults in our landing parties. We are taller than most of you, but except for that and our uniforms, we will look like very pretty Earth humans. Our children can come later, but not in the beginning because we are not willing to expose them to possible danger from whatever risks we may encounter. We will mingle among the crowds at the sites as long as it is safe to do so, and if circumstances are favorable and any in the crowds wish to board our craft, each craft commander will determine if that may be permitted.

But traveling with us is not a possibility because of the atmospheric differences in our propulsion needs and oxygen breathing on the planet. Through evolution we developed the capability to sustain breathing on two levels to accommodate our bodies when we are in spacecraft and also in atmospheres such as on Earth's surface.

Our message of peacefulness and the ways we will assist after landing have been told to your governments, but never have they publicly announced this. By laying the groundwork before the first landings, we believe it may be possible to appear on television and directly tell people around the world that we have come in peace and how we will help them and Earth.

With that, I believe I have answered all your questions, Mistress Suzy.

S: Thank you so much, Lazarus! The landings are exciting to look forward to! Is there anything else you would like to say, maybe what you feel is most important for us to know?

LAZARUS: Open your hearts and minds to God. Allow the light to flow within. Get rid of the dark forces that may be controlling you and reestablish your conscious connection directly with God. Your soul connection with God is as it has been throughout eternity, is now and evermore. KNOW your connection, LIVE your connection. Open your hearts and minds to the Oneness, the inseparability of all life in all placements throughout this universe, which God rules with love and light.

Is that sufficient for a statement of importance?

S: It's great, Lazarus, thank you. I think all your extra information will fit well in the book, don't you?

LAZARUS: Yes, we too believe this may be so, but the Council will pass on this and you will be so guided in your work. For us, it is acceptable to leave the singular and plural uses of my self and our selves as "I" and "we" varied throughout. All is covered adequately, I believe, therefore we do not anticipate being with you for another sitting, Mistress Suzy, unless we are summoned.

We commend you for your interest, your labors and your devotion to producing this essential information in book form. We are privileged to have known you thus, Mistress Suzy, and leave with wishing you well in all respects. With love and high regard, we say goodbye and look forward to meeting you in person, flesh-to-flesh, in the "future" of your counting of time. Farewell and thank you. In love, we go now. Salu.

2008:

Lazarus and I developed a warm friendship and chatted on several occasions after our conversation in 1994. Still, it was surprising that one evening a few years later, when I was in the hospital with my seriously ill daughter, he popped in and told me that she would recover completely and his "forces of energy," along with Matthew and others on and off Earth, had been beaming light to sustain her.

When I reached Lazarus' part during the revision process, he greeted me enthusiastically and we worked together to considerably shorten his original presentation. He said he welcomed the opportunity to eliminate his former "verbosity" and is extremely pleased with our joint effort that you have just read. I asked if he would like to add something about Earth's current condition from his vantage point.

LAZARUS: Thank you, Suzy, and yes, I want to give assurance that with all the in-beamed light, beloved Terra has regained a great deal of her former strength. But we still are showering her with our energy along with our technology to maintain her stability because not all the upheaval in ridding her of negativity is over, and we're not about to diminish our diligence in this respect until she is fully within fourth density vibrations and continuing her voyage to fifth. Then we'll all shout *Hallelujah!*—our work on Earth will be done and we shall return to our homeland and families.

S: But for sure, you will land and introduce your-selves and stay a while, won't you?

LAZARUS: Oh, my dear little friend, indeed "for sure" we shall! We want you to know your universal brothers and sisters! We want to teach you our technologies and assist you in returning Earth to her original paradise self—you cannot even imagine how rapidly that can be done.

S: We are SO looking forward to that! How is your family, Lazarus?

LAZARUS: Suzy, you sweet soul! My family is wonderful! Thank you for asking. I devoutly hope that when the first "ETs" make their presence known, that all people there will be able to think of us this way, with families like yours, whom we love just as dearly as you love yours.

PROMETHEUS

MATTHEW: Mother, I shall introduce to you an entity from still another origin far beyond Earth. His powerful and benevolent civilization has been given authority by God for the safekeeping of Earth's orbiting path, just as others you already have heard from. This person's name is Prometheus. Yes, I know you have heard that name before, and once again, just because of that, you are skeptical. Mother, Mother, Mother! Just please welcome Prometheus.

S: Prometheus, welcome to this sitting. I greet you in full reception to recording accurately your information if the Council has approved it for the book. So, hello!

PROMETHEUS: Hello yourself, Suzy! Thank you for that "heads-up" greeting, albeit with some reservation. My presentation has been approved, of course.

Long, long ago many visitors from outer space, as you call our worlds, came to your planet to investigate the environment for sustaining life of certain species. In time, Earth became well known as the paradise it was in those long ago times, and it became a placement of wonder, beauty and desirability in the hearts of many space explorers. You do not know of these beings yet, some of whom are not what you would think of as human, but they are nonetheless intelligent beings of great advancement in many ways beyond your conscious minds' ability to imagine. These souls are seeking their spiritual paths and are further along in their self-discovery than you in your own searching in this respect. They never will harm any soul seeking the same path and, like many other powerful sources, bring only greetings and a pledge to assist you and your planet home.

We are among these lighted beings and are the forefathers of some of your own human selves. We are from a planetary system in a constellation named Orion. There is no individual aspect of our civilization, but there is perfect harmony in the rhythmic motion of our searching ever toward the light. We have evolved into the needlessness of physical bodies, and our advancements in intelligence and spiritual truth-knowing has enabled us to materialize in thin strata formations that represent the cumulative soul essence and minds of billions of souls.

We understand that it is difficult for you to think of intelligent beings as odd cloud formations, yet we are in this appearance of proximity to Earth to exert the force required for maximum assistance. We are one of the civilizations working on behalf of your physical survival, which is one of the most important aspects of what you call "the cleansing."

It is correct to use that descriptive terminology, but the understanding of what will occur is confused by the many souls receiving information about specific stages. Some say the first stage will be heralded by a meteorite. Indeed a meteorite may hit the planet more than once with negligible effect, but the cleansing has been under way for over fifty Earth years, starting with an increase in what you call "natural disasters." These events, along with changing climates and weather patterns, will continue with increasing intensity and frequency until no one can deny that something far more dramatic than only weather oddities is happening.

In our path was placed the opportunity to be of service to your planet during these times. You do not understand the effects of foul deeds and thoughts on Mother Earth. You are only obliquely aware of these effects that set into motion the bowels of Earth up-heaving to rid the surface of the increasing heaviness of atmosphere, which is the dense negativity of mind and spirit. Not volcanic eruptions or earthquakes will take the primary toll of physical life, but the continuance of attitudes and deeds by those among you who have chosen to follow the darkness rather than the light of God. Open your hearts and thoughts to following the lighted path where wonderment abounds. This is not scripture, it is not evangelical ministry—it is truth from God directly to His children of all forms and intentions, whether on the path of darkness or of Christed light.

Our message is this: Welcome the newcomers in strange forms and from strange places. Know that among them we are foremost in sustaining the faith of your forward movement on the lighted pathway. We do not sanction fear and, in fact, we cannot approach an aura of fear as that energy is anathema to our core nature of peacefulness. We pledge our assistance in God's service and thus your own when our presence is evident above your horizon.

Welcome not only us, but all the other souls who also have declared their support for your physical and planetary safety. This is all I can persuade you to do, and it is my only purpose in addressing you this day. In the Christed light, promise and faith, I am most truly your servant in love, Prometheus of Orion.

S: Thank you, Prometheus, for your beautiful message. Are you speaking as an individual or as the spokesperson for your collective souls? Can any individual thoughts or feelings emanate from your overall soul essence?

PROMETHEUS: I have spoken as "I" as well as "we" because even as I speak for the combined souls, yet it is with a sense of individuality that I am visiting with you on this important occasion. So, indeed there can be a sensation of unity as well as individual self, but this is not often.

S: Yes, I see. When will you be undeniably evident in our skies?

PROMETHEUS: Not for at least another year of your calendar timing, more likely longer. Please remember that only a few such as yourself, who are anticipating otherworld helpers, will see anything other than frequent cloud formations in unusual configurations. The clouds will be your stratus-cirrus variety with "puffs" where an energy vortex is required to lessen the intensity of pollution from the chemicals and other toxins in your soil, water and atmosphere. That pollution comes from the thoughts and deeds of dark ones, as I said. May I answer further for you?

S: Yes, please. Are you cooperating with other extraterrestrial forces or will your effort be restricted to your own powers, and how long will you be helping us? When will the cleansing process be completed, and what will the configuration be then of the planet's earth and sea masses?

PROMETHEUS: We will be working along with but not in unity with other powers from far beyond your planet. We will remain as long as the stabilizing forces provided by us and others are necessary to keep Earth orbiting regularly and your polar areas from tilting so drastically and far afield of current placement that an instant ice age would befall Earth.

As for completion time of the cleansing, we cannot say as that is a process in motion. We can say that the large land and sea changes on the map called "I am America" are not now as accurate as they once were. With awakenings of Earth souls and more benevolence in some areas of former hatred and evildoing, there is diminishing need for that scale of stabilizing, or balancing, the energy currents. But lower, darker energies have increased in other areas that will require considerable help in that respect.

There will be many "natural disasters," as you call them, but not all are coming from Earth's own efforts to survive. Some of these events are being manipulated by technology in the hands of dark souls on the planet. Nevertheless, the energy releases assist Earth in up-righting her orbit, eventually without the aid of our combined forces to sustain energy alignment.

Death, as your word is, of many people and animals will be unavoidable, but the transition from physical life to the next stage of the soul's development is only a momentary step and not to be feared. Transition comes to each soul at the appropriate time, according to the choice in the soul's contract made prior to birth.

S: Thank you for your courtesy in replying so extensively. Will you return for another sitting?

PROMETHEUS: It is not our plan to do so as there is nothing more I can tell you or am authorized to tell you. So I believe bidding you goodbye with love in the lighted worship of God is our final word.

S: Goodbye then, and thank you, Prometheus.

2008:

S: Prometheus? Am I right in thinking that you are here?

PROMETHEUS: You are indeed, Suzy! Just as you are wondering now about my presence, often you look up at the sky and wonder if we are present. Oh yes, we are in full force as the need is great for our energy to reduce or neutralize to the greatest extent possible the quantity of toxins abounding everywhere around you. It is impossible for you to breathe pure air or for your marine life to live in pure waters, and even the organically grown produce cannot escape the proliferation of pollutants. But with our assistance and others' as well, the prevalent pollution is not nearly as damaging as it would be otherwise.

The cleansing is not yet in final stages, but the headway is close to miraculous from the first moments when Earth cried out for assistance. We are privileged and honored to be in the forefront of this cleansing effort insofar as our nearness to you. We maneuver around the skies in search of toxic trails to dissolve so the particles that fall to Earth's surface carry less damaging elements. We still are reducing the pollutants in the seas as well, but this effort is more discouraging because of the sonic currents that are so harmful to life there. And we impart our energy to other forces on the ground to give them invisibility as protection in times of danger.

So you see, we are very much in your midst! And
joyfully so, as the years between our first talk and now
have produced such great enlightenment and uplifted
spirits among the populace! All of us in your "space"
community of families look forward with great anticipa-
tion to introducing ourselves in a form that you will see
at first with amazement and then embrace as the brothers
and sisters we all are. The lighted pathway is leading to
grand excitement as the Golden Age of Earth is nearing!

Now, my friend Suzy, I see no more questions in
your mind, so I shall say "Adieu" for this moment, but
remember that I am as close as your thought of me.

*S: And that is a most heartwarming thought,
Prometheus! Thank you for coming, and now I say
"Adieu" to you.*

AGNES

S: *Welcome, Agnes. Thank you for coming to offer information to the people of Earth.*

AGNES: This is my privilege, Suzanne of Matthew's energy. For simplicity I shall address you as Suzanne, if I may. I am ready to transmit a message of importance to Earth. I greet you in peacefulness and attentiveness to the needs of Earth consciousness in all its radiance of her Beginnings as paradise.

Long pause...

S: *Your energy is lovely, Agnes. Will you tell me, please, why and how you wish to assist Earth?*

AGNES: We are in peace and love witnessing the travail of your beautiful Earth. No longer has she the beauty on the surface or the interior due to the negative enactments of the civilizations that have inhabited this planet for eons, so far back in antiquity that you have only deeply submerged memory of that time.

My civilization was partly responsible for the populating of Earth in its earliest seedings. We always have held most dear not only the humans living within this atmosphere, but that paradise of a homeland selected for your breeding and experiencing. It was intended that someday we would reunite with you in all glory and recognition, but there has been no attempt on your part to encourage such a reunion. This is from fear and loss of memory, and it does not change our relationship, it does not lessen our love and brotherhood. So that tells you most clearly why we are here at this time of severe changes.

We will assist in ways individual rather than collective. That is, our focus is on souls as individuals, not on the population of Earth in entirety. Other entities already present will assist in such ways as stability of orbit and extra energy beaming into the atmosphere for leveling upwards the cellular memories. We are not needed in this respect. Although, if so needed, we stand at the forefront of those lines of assistance with our love beaming as a deterrent to massive Earth shifts in the nature of destruction of our brothers.

Our purpose is to reunite with those souls who came from our own beginnings. All souls here are precious in God's regard, so we do not denigrate one soul and uplift another arbitrarily. It is as if a family on Earth called in the cousins and aunts and uncles so all are under the grandparents' roof for reunion. It is a natural selection, is it not, and you do not feel it is necessary to invite all who may pass by the roadway beyond? So it is with our mission and purpose. Yes, of God, in all ways and always.

We will approach not in our form, as the welcoming parties are rarely happy to see a stranger in the kitchen. First, we are already with you. Second, some of you have seen us in radiance, recognized in an energy that is warm and embracing. The recognition is not as a brother to a brother, but as a sense of wonderment and smoothness of the experience. Deeply, yes, this is indeed brother to brother, but at the surface level where you are thinking most of the time there is only wonderment at the sensations that are coming with greater recognition and frequency.

And what do we accomplish by this means? Reunion pathway. Hand in hand on a deep level we are walking with you toward the light. This is toward junctions you will recognize at soul level, a sense of familiarity without explanation, and later with conscious memory that will be welcomed, however startling. It will be the *"Aha!"* from your soul.

Nevertheless, not all connections will be made as wished, even though this happening I just related would indeed be joyous for each of you and for us. Not all of you with whom we are being in these times will feel anything akin to my description. Some of you will choose to stay mired in the dream of self that you have created out of experiencing at superficial degrees of reality. Often these experiences have little to do with the reality of the soul's purpose for this embodiment because the pathway has been so far wandered from as to provide experiences *not* chosen prior to the embodiment.

Yes, you are lost. And when we tap into your hearts and minds to give you a tiny spark of light to follow, often you do not wish to make that deviation from the path you have carved for yourselves. This is a disappointment for us, but it is not our place to do more than be the spark. We cannot drag or push you into seeking the spark.

So then, why now? Why not in prior years? Or, why this soon are we attempting to reunite? You, I believe, are unprepared to believe this planet will be changing in great ways that will have profound effects on its surface. The seas will move forcibly into lowlands and flood cities in those lands. In the plains Earth will rise into mountains and valleys will be formed between. Other places, where now mountains stand tall with snow peaks, will tumble and create canyons of great depth and length. Water will change its pace and salinity as the polar areas melt and re-form. There will be skies of long darkness, as the sun may be swept from your vision by the dust arising into the atmosphere, then of long light in this process. The clearing will be many days, many years, while the settlement of the lands and seas rests finally into place.

That is why we are here now. We have been here before, as I said. We will not abandon you after the changes. But now is a critical time of reassessing your pathway. It is a lamp that we bring to you to light your way back to the Oneness. In God we find selves, always! But first we must recognize that God is within each soul. There is not a massive being of strong opinions and strict rules, as your churches often portray. The God within is our connection in family, our connection in soul and love and the lighted way to unity.

We are here to be your guides, if you so wish. Yes, we have chosen those among you whom we will guide, if desired, if permitted, because you are our family and many others are not. There are among our family many millions, however, and there are other progenitors such as ourselves whose families also will be contacted in the same way as we are now reaching our own.

For you who are reading this book, you may or may not be one of our soulmates in family lineage. But you are one of the souls whose progenitors are holding out a spiritual hand to guide, if you will but take it. God's assigned missions to us are to reach all souls who will greet us. We may never be seen in a dense form, or we may, but do not doubt that we are present in all strength and willingness to walk hand in hand with you until your basic memory has returned and you will welcome the companion along the journey to the LIGHT.

In God's homelands of mansions untold in glory, we serve. In God's love we send this message to all people of Earth. Farewell, in glory.

During Agnes' transmission, I felt as if I were not separate from her but rather wafting within her energy, which was like a gentle sea of golden fluid. Later Matthew told me that he and I are of the same ancient civilization as she—our Earth lives started with her group's seeding program. Apparently my soul level awareness of reunion was so strong that it produced my unique sense of merging with her.

Agnes didn't send me an image of herself and I had no opportunity to question her after the presentation, but with her farewell, she left a distinct and lingering floral fragrance.

2008:

As I was reading Agnes' message while working on this revised edition, I felt the same gentle energy I did 14 years ago. I was simply enjoying this sensation when Agnes spoke: *"And now, dear soul Suzanne, you understand."* She said it is extremely gratifying to her people that many of their Earth family are responding to the love energy surrounding them. She went on to say that the extent of changes she described in her message has diminished tenfold during the interim years, with thanks to the joint efforts of light workers on Earth and helpers in our universal community. *"All the heavens await your self-recognition as multidimensional souls."*

PART VII

CREATOR'S DECREE

THE DECREE

In autumn 1995 Matthew told me that the dark forces had been stepping up their negativity bombardment of Earth to counter the light beings' increased activities on our behalf. Telepathic communication lines between Nirvana and Earth were being reinforced with additional light energy to prevent incursion by the dark forces. During sittings from that time for the next six or eight months, Matthew was in the company of about 100 souls whose composite energy enabled our unbroken contact.

Often the transmissions during that period, including the one that follows, were from the "group mind," the knowledge of all the participating individuals amalgamated by a universal synthesis process. When Matthew spoke alone he was supported by the group's collective energy. In either case, I was addressed as Mother.

October 17, 1995:

MATTHEW/GROUP: Mother, we greet you this morning with MOMENTOUS news! Creator has decreed that no longer may the peak of the dark forces use its free will to hold captive the free will of any other soul! We wish you could know the rejoicing of all spiritually evolved beings throughout this universe when this news was related by Creator's messengers!

I shall explain why this decree is a glorious victory of unprecedented scope for the light forces. By Creator's rule, the free will choices of every light being always have been and always shall be honored. However, the peak of darkness has ignored this rule and used its free will to capture the free will of every soul who developed "evil" tendencies. That kept strengthening the energy of the dark forces and making its combined free will power far greater than the free will of each individual light being. And that is why for eons the darkness was able to create negativity throughout this universe and the free will of individual light beings was unable to stop it.

In accordance with Creator's decree, God has withdrawn that abuse of free will from the dark forces in this universe and released all of its captive souls. Now that the free will of ALL souls can be honored, the former lopsided battle between the light and the dark is over!

The most profound effect on Earth is this: The cleansing to rid your planet of the mass of accumulated negativity can be far less in scope and intensity than would have been necessary prior to the decree. When the cleansing activity began about half a century ago, intense negativity still was building and the very existence of your planet was in dire jeopardy. The light that was needed to save Earth's body also was needed to restructure her human residents' cellular make-up, a DNA "upgrading" that is done at soul level and is essential for both spiritual clarity and physical survival in the higher densities where Earth is heading.

The restructuring could have been completed within a twinkling of your eye, but it still is in process because the battle between light and dark not only prevented that swiftness, but the darkness kept adding to negativity's tremendous pressures that keep at low level the consciousness of Earth's peoples. Throughout the past five decades, the light being beamed from powerful off-planet sources has been relieving the negativity.

Without that immensity of incoming light, the dark forces could have been successful in their intention to capture all souls on Earth, but thanks to the light forces, now that isn't even a possibility!

However, even though the darkness no longer has the power of the combined free will of its captive souls, its influence during their long confinement cannot be abruptly shaken. By their thoughts, feelings and actions—along with the same from all other individuals who have dark tendencies—they still are generating negativity. That will gradually fade until Earth's population will be only souls living within the light.

Until Earth has rid herself of all negativity, its release through geophysical upheavals will continue. Many unseen helpers will lessen the damage and death toll—in addition to the powerful light being beamed by highly evolved civilizations, their advanced technology will level out the effects of earthquakes, volcanic eruptions and violent storms. Among these civilizations, Mother, are those whose representatives sent you their cogent messages for Earth's people.

S: Matthew, your news about Creator's decree and what it means to Earth is beyond my ability to express! But will the presentations by the other civilizations have the same value now?

MATTHEW/GROUP: ABSOLUTELY, Mother! For decades those souls have been helping to save Earth's very life and breath! It is virtually unknown on the planet that only the intervention of your benevolent space family kept Earth in stable orbit throughout her long struggle to recover from death throes. Although the cleansing won't need to be as cataclysmic as formerly thought, people of Earth need to know the steadfast willingness of those civilizations to keep assisting in whatever measure is needed! Furthermore, their inestimable help is as vital now as before, because the darkness views Earth's souls as a prize to be won or lost, and in its fervor to win, it is increasing its tactical armaments of fear, chaos, lies, confusion, divisiveness and violence.

So absolutely yes, Mother, those messages have the same critical importance now as before Creator's decree! Knowing that you are members of our universal family and knowing about the assistance that many have been giving Earth is paramount in raising the mass consciousness so you do not fall prey to the wiliness of the dark ones! Spiritually evolved souls throughout this universe devoutly wish that this ongoing assistance become known with gratitude and that you will joyously welcome your brothers and sisters in the spirit of loving and open cooperation. Mother, the messages you received will help pave the way.

S: Yes, I see that now, dear. Besides the reduction in drastic cleansing, what is in store for us?

MATTHEW/GROUP: At individual level, the duality within each soul—the personal karmic choices to achieve the balance necessary for soul evolvement and reintegration with God—will be successfully resolved. Long hidden truths will come forth, such as each of you is an inseparable part of God and all other souls, and telepathic communication is your birthright. These and many other truths will come in increments during the next several years as the power of the light keeps intensifying and reaches hearts and minds. Not all souls will be receptive and that is all right—they will have other lifetime opportunities to embrace the light.

Many changes will come about in governments at all levels as the corrupt and tyrannical leaders are replaced by persons with wisdom and spiritual integrity. This process also will take several years because there will be strong opposition from the current leaders and those who follow in their dark footsteps, but eventually the light will prevail in such intensity that the power of the dark ones simply will cease to exist.

Your monetary systems will change. Not need, but *greed* is the basis of commerce and the entire economy of Earth—with that core of darkness, those systems cannot survive as the light keeps increasing. When honor is returned to all means of goods and services exchange, what serves the good of all will be the new standards.

The many sources of mind control, which are pervasive in your world by design of the dark masters, will be reduced, then eliminated as people "see the light." Those who have just been released from the hold of darkness lost the ability to use conscience during their captivity; that ability is being returned and fortified by the infusion of light to assist them in using their newly returned free will in positive ways.

In summary, Mother, all measures designed to keep people in ignorance, deception, fear and misery will end when the last of the darkness is transmuted into light. A transformation of this magnitude cannot happen overnight, and we urge everyone on Earth to rejoice in the awareness that all along your exhilarating journey into the Golden Age, lighted souls throughout the universe will be your loving and helpful travel companions!

PART VIII

CONTROVERSIES

ABORTION

S: Matthew, you've said that Nirvana has souls who monitor everything that happens here, but do you form opinions about our controversial issues or do you consider that making judgments?

MATTHEW: Well, Mother, we're not all that different from you that we would not have opinions of your situations, but having an opinion is not the same as judging the individuals involved! I see where you're going with this, but please write it for the record.

S: OK. What's your opinion of abortion?

MATTHEW: Ending the lives of unborn babies is a clear-cut issue here—it eliminates opportunities for souls to embody. However, there is no condemnation of any woman who chooses not to allow the birth. Often this is part of a pre-birth agreement, with the abortion and the emotional adjustment to it being lessons chosen by the souls of both the mother and the fetus.

Because of the negativity this subject has created, there is more concern here about the pressure directed by some people against those who favor allowing women to make their own decisions about a birth or an abortion. The ostensible motive of those who are adamantly anti-abortion is to save unborn lives, but the underlying motive is their wish to control others, and it is this nature far more than it is one of saving a potential life that drives them to engage in public protests. Usually

this is not consciously realized by those individuals or
the general population, but an indication that you can
observe is the protesters' lack of providing nurturing,
financial help or protection for the unwanted babies who
are born due to their pressure.

There is no judgment here of any of these people, not
those who perform the abortions or those who have them
or those who protest them. This furor is part of the dark
forces' strategic "prophecy" of "widespread killing," and it
is a necessary stage of experiencing for everyone who is
affected.

*S: You said a fetus has a soul—what happens to the
soul in case of abortion?*

MATTHEW: A soul may enter the fetus in full awareness that it may be aborted. Often a soul is present in the
general area of an imminent pregnancy because it wants to
absorb the energies of the environment and the potential
parents. A soul may want this experience even when
there is the likelihood or even assurance that if conception
occurs, the outcome will be an abortion.

The fetus is aware of nothing beyond its own sensation
of existence. The soul that enters it may choose to do so
fully or only as a short-time caretaker in the case of an
anticipated abortion or stillbirth. In some cases the souls
are willing to have a potentially short experiencing
because they are hopeful that the fetus will be allowed to
develop into an infant. When it is a foregone conclusion
that will not happen, a soul still may choose to have that
brief physical existence.

Generally that choice is based on its primary effect,
which is emotional. It is a restful period for the fetus in
moments of total peacefulness insofar as physical

sensations, and the other side of this picture also contributes to the soul emotionally. An unwanted pregnancy usually causes severe emotional conflict prior to a planned abortion, and all of that energy is absorbed by the fetus to the extent that it could serve as a substitute for the same experiencing during a physical lifetime.

If all of this were known to everyone on Earth, abortion would not be a religious, legal, political or even a controversial issue.

2008:

S: Hi dear! Now that I'm at this point in revising for foreign editions, I'm thinking that stem cell research using discarded embryos is OK from the viewpoint in Nirvana.

MATTHEW: Mother, the darkest minds on Earth are prohibiting that kind of research by making it part and parcel of the anti-abortion movement, thereby evoking the huge outcry against it. In the minds of many others, it is unconscionable to legally forbid the development of methods that can prevent or cure diseases that cause misery and pain to so many people.

This is a prime example of opposing sides creating the energy attachments that keep them widely divided. The energy generated by the universal law of "like attracts like" never ends its pursuit of adherents, and only by decreasing efforts to seek "like," can you decrease energy's momentum. The vehemence of the "for" and "against" sides in this research issue is feeding that momentum and preventing rational discussion of ways to benevolently use and protect against the abuse of discoveries.

BIRTH CONTROL

S: Is your attitude about birth control similar to your feelings about abortion, that it eliminates opportunities for souls to embody?

MATTHEW: No, we do not feel similarly about birth control. Earth is not meant to be only a breeding ground for souls to incarnate! How many people can your planet support in its unhealthy condition? How many children can be cared for by the same parents, with diligent attention and provision of all life's basic needs? How many orphaned children can find their way without the security of parental love and supervision in those countries where the birthrate is high, living conditions are deplorable and longevity rate is low? Many children are abandoned, left to fend for themselves. Birth control is sensible!

While some souls do choose emotional turmoil, poverty and substandard living conditions to balance previous lifetimes, due to the intense suffering of the billions affected, those widespread conditions are generating far more negativity than they are fulfilling selected karmic lessons. There is more than enough negativity on Earth for those people to endure, and no great numbers of souls here are eager to embody in those areas where highest birth rates are prevailing! Negativity caused by undue suffering needs to be dissipated and spirits healed rather than subjecting greater numbers of babies to it.

Most people who are educated in birth control measures approve of this means of family planning, even those who devoutly observe other aspects of religious dogmas. In countries with little availability of education or contraceptive products, mothers are disheartened by more pregnancies when they cannot properly care for their little children in the impoverished, and often tyrannical, conditions or fathers cannot be present to assist. Those sentiments are not held exclusively by those mothers, of course, but there is more despair among them than in countries where contraceptives are available.

We see positive results for your world when sensitive, sensible and loving parents choose not to have more children than they can attend with love, wisdom and guidance, and contraception is the most effective means of achieving this.

S: Do you think China's policy about one child per family is practical?

MATTHEW: We cannot endorse any restriction or denial of individuals' free will. If one child is by the parents' choice rather than the mandate of some "authority," we would view this in gladness for those families.

S: Do you think the easy availability of contraceptives has promoted sexual promiscuity among teenagers, or do you not think about things like this?

MATTHEW: Mother, we think about whatever you do—we have much more awareness of your lives than you imagine! Not by sticking in our noses, but through your invitation by your thoughts of us or simply the awareness here of thoughts generally prevailing on Earth.

So yes, we know that many of you believe that the accessibility of contraceptives is encouraging sexual relations among young people, but availability of anything does not promote or guarantee either its use or abuse— it is a matter only of one's free will choice! Consider the many people who know how beneficial exercising, healthful eating and meditation are for body, mind and spirit, yet your population as a whole is not clamoring to incorporate those into their lifestyle. Regardless of all the blatant advertising of "sexiness" in everything from shampoos to vehicles, sexual activity is a matter of *choice.*

What is at stake regarding all issues you consider "social problems" is the eroded foundation of human will and the lack of cooperative, harmonious and nonjudgmental attitudes among family, neighbors, co-workers. Extend that into communities, cities and nations and you can see that humankind is suffering from a lack of spiritual awareness of their inseparable connection with God and each other. The many publicized reasons for teenage promiscuity and other types of behavior you call "social problems" don't include the root cause—the influence of the darkness that wants to keep you ignorant of your inseparable soul connections. As more and more of you awaken to the truth of your god and goddess selves, you will live in consonance with your awakened consciousness and conscience.

CAPITAL PUNISHMENT

S: What is the opinion there of capital punishment?

MATTHEW: The "legal" killing of any person is not in God's eyes a just act. It does not correct a murderous killing, it is a new commission of the very same kind of act. The latter act is legally defined as "justice" and the murderous act as "wrongful," but they are equally wrong.

S: Matthew, life in prison rather than execution would protect society from convicted murderers, but it doesn't seem fair that someone who has sadistically tortured and killed maybe several people would get the same punishment as someone who did kill, but without that same intent or brutality. So can you recommend another way?

MATTHEW: Recommendations originating anywhere except in your own world would not be effective, Mother. We can only hope—pray!—for eyes to be opened unto what could be called the eyes of God so you can see that especially in this time of accelerated learning, when the time for experiencing chosen lessons is rapidly diminishing, capital punishment is not in the best interests of *anyone!*

To be sure, it is necessary to remove violent criminals from further opportunities to torture or kill. Confinement accomplishes this, and it will be necessary only as an interim measure until the elimination of such behavior on Earth comes to pass, and it shall. The light being beamed into human hearts and minds increasingly will lessen the need for prisons because there will be less and less desire in anyone to harm others.

The lessening would happen much more quickly if the opposing sides regarding capital punishment were de-emphasized. That is, if there were less support for legalized execution, those who oppose it could lessen their outcry for it to cease. With the abatement of the opposing energy streamers, there would be less "fuel" to continue the divisive opinions, and that fuel is horrible crimes.

As to what is "fair" punishment, your prisons are confining great numbers of people whose actions created insignificant negativity in comparison with the massive negativity caused by their collective emotions during and after the term of incarceration. All too often imprisonment and even execution results from a wrongful verdict of guilt. Unjust—even inhumane!—laws, poor defense of the accused, arbitrary application of legal technicalities, and deceit and corruption are rampant in nations' law enforcement and "justice" systems. Like all other situations in your world that are rooted in darkness, this too will end.

PHYSICIAN-ASSISTED SUICIDE

S: After hearing your opinion of capital punishment, I'm assuming you don't approve of physician-assisted suicide, either.

MATTHEW: You know the trouble with assumptions, Mother! We see that this matter is indeed adamantly controversial there, but in this realm no controversy exists at all APPROVAL here is the most significant reason for its emergence there! But clearly we do not think of this in the same way you do, considering the name you have given to what actually is a means of divine grace whereby the dying person's psyche is released from further trauma.

The physician sees his patient's inability to deal much longer with intractable pain and incapacitation, and he knows that no medication or treatment can restore even a minimum quality of life. For the patient's psyche to adjust to a deteriorating physical condition, there must be a sense of at least partial enjoyment, productivity and learning; when that sense of any meaningful life is gone, so is the desire to retain the existing minimal life force.

The psyche of a person who endures intense physical and emotional suffering along with seeing the anguish of loved ones, experiences the damage equivalent of wartime or torture trauma, and the psyche arrives here in that same shattered condition. The long-term treatment required to restore its functioning ability considerably delays the person's adjustment to life in this realm.

Avoiding or lessening the need for that lengthy restoration process is to be devoutly wished, and what you have termed "physician-assisted suicide" helps to alleviate that need.

What we see is that often the people who request assistance to end their physical life have outlived their pre-birth agreement. They have suffered unduly longer or have lived beyond the point of debility agreed upon, and forced continuation of the body's feeble viability is neither helpful nor desirable at either conscious or soul levels. That is why peacefulness comes within these people when their decision to end the lifetime with a physician's help is allowed to be honored. This would be much more correctly termed "physician-assisted transition."

We do not look favorably upon a committee deciding whether to permit the free will decisions of the patient and the physician. The same sentiment applies to any group trying to dictate to others how they should think, feel or act. In this realm always there is less sympathy with "outsiders" who feel they have the judgment ability, the responsibility, and even the right to interfere in situations not in agreement with their own views. Those people would be better served if they practice their philosophies within their groups of adherents and extend that same right of choice to all others.

ORGAN TRANSPLANTS

S: *How are human organ transplants regarded in Nirvana, Matthew?*

MATTHEW: If organ transplantation were not beneficial to people on Earth, the medical technology would not have been filtered to your physicians from the universe, where the thought forms already existed. Your physical bodies are only very temporary vehicles for your souls. When the soul departs from a body it no longer needs, any healthy parts successfully transplanted into a body struggling for viability can offer greatly improved life quality and longevity to the recipient.

What cannot be known is the soul contract of the person who receives the body parts. That is, transplantation failure may result because of the person's pre-birth agreement that includes experiencing the physical condition or death, and the failure is not due to transplant surgery that may be deemed to have been poorly performed or any subsequent treatment deemed deficient.

It is true that organ transplantation can be abused— anything designed in goodness can be used in ungodly ways!—however, with ethical care and diligence, any attempt at abuse is greatly minimized. It also is true that people have been killed specifically for the sale of their organs. These ungodly happenings, like other vile abuses of free will on Earth, will end as the light keeps intensifying and the darkness in humankind is transmuted into light.

VACCINES

*S: Matthew, do you know that some medical
researchers think vaccines may be the cause of autism?*

MATTHEW: Oh, we are very well aware of this,
Mother, but true autism is what I described some time
ago, a rare condition that a soul chooses to balance other
lifetimes. Medical researchers are finding that vaccines
can indeed be far more harmful than helpful, and some
have linked their effects to autism. It is so that the
symptoms are similar to autism, but what doctors do *not*
know is that the vaccines are meant to produce those
effects.

Some vaccines have been developed *specifically* to
cause problems! Their original intent was to preserve life
by eradicating disease—now the intent is to eradicate life
by causing disease. This is just one more example of the
work of the dark forces. It takes only a handful of darkly-
influenced minds—the ones who conceive the ideas and
their cohorts who develop or contaminate some vaccines—
to carry out this sinister plot. Vaccinations are not
voluntary in many cases. They are mandated by
unsuspecting authorities who simply follow orders given
to them, and severe repercussions befall the dissenters.
So inoculations are administered by well-meaning health
caregivers who are unaware that they are *infecting*, not
protecting, people.

You can see evidence of this in the viruses that are
prevalent on Earth. The most pernicious of these, which
causes what you call AIDS, is a skillfully designed

combination of mutant viruses that comes directly from a laboratory to achieve the purpose it is fulfilling. How foolish to state that AIDS originated in monkeys! If that were the case, you must question how the disease was so easily traced to them when they aren't affected by it as humans are. And since the virus isn't airborne, how could the first individuals diagnosed with AIDS have been bitten by infected monkeys? That disease wasn't discovered in the countries where the monkeys live—it appeared in homosexual individuals who lived in two cities on opposite coasts of a continent thousands of miles away! We can only wonder why, when people now are clamoring for the truth about many other "official" stories, they are not questioning the true origin of AIDS.

Beyond the millions who are suffering and the death toll that keeps mounting are many other sources of negativity stemming from this disease: the physical and emotional pain and hopelessness of the ill and their families; the grief and hardships of survivors; the many children orphaned; the fear of the vastness to which this "incurable" disease has spread, debilitating entire nations' peoples. By dark design, the vaccines and later, the "treatment" medications, created all this negativity, and the misery and grief so far exceeds the experiencing chosen by the affected individuals as to be indescribable.

Mother, I know I digressed far afield from your question about autism and once again attributed a situation to the darkness—and rightly so, because darkness is the root of ALL types of suffering, despair and devastation in your world!—but the truth about vaccines needs to be known so this horrendous situation can be ended for once and for all!

2008:

I will tell you why the more recent laboratory-made viruses called SARS and avian flu did not result in the pandemics that they also were intended to become. You may remember the enormous amount of fear-filled international publicity about each disease in turn, with the alarm that it could reach pandemic proportions; that vaccines were suspiciously quickly available and widely distributed; that headlines blared each new diagnosis— and eventually all that hoopla disappeared because there were so few instances of illness or death. Earth, who is a sentient being and whose soul grieved over the dark intent of the designers of those viruses, did not want those diseases to cause millions of her residents to suffer and die; and in honoring her free will choice, God authorized civilizations with advanced technology to neutralize those viruses.

2009:

Mother, let me take this opportunity of your final review to add a bit here because now Earth's peoples are being subjected to the second go-round of the swine flu pandemic. This time it has a different designation (H1N1) and billions of vials of vaccines with the virus and other, more toxic ingredients are being prepared for worldwide distribution. The new element this time is widespread protests decrying the World Health Organization's pressure for mandatory inoculations against a flu that has mild symptoms.

At this point we don't know if that outcry will result in the mandate's rescission—in Earth's energy field of potential, the energy of the protesters is about equal to the energy of the powerful dark minds that are determined to pursue this course. They are pinning their hopes on mandatory inoculations to produce a gargantuan amount of fear, many millions of deaths, and many billions of dollars to add to their bottomless coffers. Even if the mandate holds, the same means that rendered vaccines worthless in the prior two pandemic attempts has been used here too, and the end result will be another defeat for the darkness.

ADDICTIONS

S: The harmful effects of alcohol and illegal drugs are obvious, but do they have any effects that aren't?

MATTHEW: Indeed they do! Their combined effects are not confined to the imbalance in bodies and damaged brains of users, or even their death and the grief of their families. Or the distressing behavior or crimes stemming from drugs, or the drug-related prison populations, or the corruption and greed and ruthlessness of those who profit from the illegal drug industry in amounts you would find inconceivable.

All of that indeed produces rampant negativity, but the most vicious effect of drugs, which includes alcohol, is the chemical barrier they form between the consciousness and the soul. This barrier reduces the users' ability to absorb light, which is essential for achieving balance. How often have I stressed that balance is imperative to a soul's evolution! Now you can see why the darkly-inclined ones are so eager to keep curiosity about the "highs" ever growing and addiction to drug use permanent.

In no way do I mean that addicted persons are working in league with the dark forces! However, because heavy drug users' light and balance are greatly diminished, they are useful to the forces' aim of extinguishing all light on the planet. One person's reduction in those critical elements correspondingly resonates into the universe, and when you consider the numbers of drug-dependent people on Earth today, you can see that the total is a significant coup for the darkness.

S: What about addictive prescription drugs?

MATTHEW: Most assuredly addiction is not restricted to "illegal" drugs, and even those medications that are not physiologically addictive can easily become emotional crutches. Just as it is with so much on Earth that originated in good intent, which medicine was, now pharmaceuticals are being developed and used in such profusion that it is stunning even to us.

Drugstore shelves overflow with chemicals—even synthetic forms of natural substances—that may partially relieve one condition while creating other unhealthy conditions. The widespread consumption of medications is NOT good for you—their chemicals greatly hamper and may even destroy your bodies' self-healing mechanisms. It is solely in the best interests of the pharmaceutical companies for people to try every "over-the-counter" drug available that may or may not give momentary help, or to unquestioningly follow a doctor's prescription.

It is especially sad to see the large numbers of children being drugged because of behavior that often is due to circumstances over which they have no control or even awareness. Harmful food additives and the inescapable toxic pollution, including the very harmful manmade wavelengths, along with planetary changes in this unique time are impacting bodies, minds and spirits. Adults also are reacting in pronounced ways that they don't understand either.

The higher frequencies prevailing are magnifying all characteristics and emotions—in simplest terms, "good" is getting better and "bad" is getting worse—and changes in temperament, stress level and behavior are natural reactions to the new energies. The "tranquilizing" medications that are being consumed in such quantity as to be a chemical pandemic are especially risky—they alter brainwaves and intensify the effects of the combination of toxic pollutants and the higher frequencies that Earth has reached in her steady ascension progress.

S: Do you have any advice for overcoming addictions?

MATTHEW: The key is wholehearted desire to overcome the addiction. This begins with one's self-honesty, admitting "I am addicted" to self, which is very difficult because the intended effect of drugs is denial that they are a problem even as the user's life is centered around the next "fix." If people truly understood prayer and the power of prayer, they could use this to overcome their drug dependency. No power on Earth is greater than the light, and the light energy in prayer is inestimable! Prayer is not kneeling in public humility or even in private—it is one's innate connection with God in thoughts and feelings, anywhere, anytime. In a calm, quiet way, ask for help: "Help me overcome my need for drugs" or "Give me the strength to stop drinking" or any other few words that are comfortable. The longings of the heart speak equally clearly to God.

Of course, the dark forces don't intend that anyone dependent upon drugs desire any help to forego its use. The weakened will and reasoning of the person due to decreased light within cannot permit recognition of his problem. This is an intended inherent effect of drugs! Consequently, the spiritual supportiveness of family and friends is essential, and the same from a rehabilitation clinic with proven success may be necessary. Visualizing the user in radiant health surrounded by light can be effective for both self-help and all in the supportive group. Visualizing light around and permeating oneself and others—and Earth as well!—is wondrously uplifting and healing.

Various methods of "alternative" health care can effectively reduce or eliminate dependence upon chemical medications, and the holistic therapies that include one's approach to life offer great benefits. Changing a negative outlook to positive is especially beneficial in helping one achieve balance in mind, body and spirit— *balance is optimum health!*

Preoccupation with gambling, sexual activity, unnatural eating habits or any other obsession also is addiction. Individuals indulging in those activities can become seriously unbalanced—once again, the importance of balance cannot be overstated!—and my suggestions for overcoming drug addiction apply equally to those kinds of behavior.

GUNS

S: You must know that gun control is very controversial, and I'm curious about the opinion of guns in Nirvana.

MATTHEW: Mother, it is charming to see your head totally blank for a change. Often you have at least a vague idea of what I will tell you about a new topic based upon my replies to other topics. Sometimes you're right, sometimes close, sometimes way off, as you know. Anyway, you may or may not be surprised to know that there is no opposition here to guns. They are precisely designed and crafted and are gracefully balanced in their parts, and there is admiration for the skill and talent that designed the finest classes of these, just as there is for any finely produced item.

Our vehement opposition is to gun *use*. Guns have been one of the most misused of all items ever manifested on Earth by the thought forms of the civilization. In the beginning the purpose was the easier killing of animals for food, and the idea of how that could be achieved led to accessing matching thought forms in the universe, so the invention was rooted in beneficial use. However, so rapidly as to be a wink in even Earth time calculations, the misuse began. It has accelerated to the extent that the very existence of guns has paralyzed part of your population and incited another part to obtain guns to fulfill the fears of the first group. This is the magnified energy of fear at work as well as the balancing aspect of Earth's third density polarity, and the combination is literally lethal.

It is not sensible to fear an item that by itself has no thought, no action and no consequence. We are back once more to the weakened will, judgment and conscience of people who lack the spiritual clarity of their God connection. Since we've talked at length about this connection, about balance and about the dark forces and the light, you can easily see how and why guns have been brought into the picture. Did the dark forces design guns? No. Did they motivate persons lacking light to extend gun use from killing for food to killing humans? Yes.

As times and minds on Earth changed, aims and the methods of achieving those aims kept pace. Imagine your world today if suddenly all guns disappeared. Wars without guns—how else would the troops fight as effectively? Or gangs without guns—what other weapons could they use as easily? Or persons with deadly criminal minds—what else would serve them as well as guns? But find options they would if guns abruptly disappeared, because the psychic conditioning of combat troops, gang members and deranged killers would *not* be changed.

The populace that defends gun ownership sees only that people are the issue, not guns. The opposing side sees that if there were no proliferation of guns, the shooting would stop. Despite what I just said about that psychic hold on people, both sides in this issue are naïve. There is most decidedly a middle ground here. It is the leveling of the opposing forces into the balance that every situation needs so the two sides can stop their intense seesawing, but neither side in this issue sees any merit in the other's argument. If the two sides would subdue their outcries, both would benefit. Your planet would benefit! I told you that the fuel keeping alive your capital punishment controversy is violent crimes—this fervent issue about guns provides the very same kind of fuel.

We understand that many want guns to protect their homes and families or business sites from intruders, and others feel guns are necessary to defend the populace from forces who wish to dominate all peoples of all nations. But the means to eliminate threats to life and freedom is *not* weapons. It is the light that is beaming more and more steadily into the receptive souls of Earth humankind to bring about the leveling of all intense controversial issues now raging there. However, your temperance of attitude toward guns can hasten that day when there will be no desire of anyone to threaten, kill or dominate another.

S: *With so many issues where there is adamant disagreement, no wonder there's so much anger. It may be part of human nature, just like love and pleasantness, but those traits are much nicer to have around.*

MATTHEW: I agree that love and pleasantness are far nicer than anger in any circumstance, Mother, but it is not correct that love is part of human nature as you see it—someone who is amiable or is not. Love is an integral component of the lighted soul essence with a boundless capacity for feeling and expressing, and it is much different from pleasantness and other learned characteristics or behavior a person develops, which lumped together are the "personality."

Anger also may be seen as a personality trait, but actually it, too, is a soul level capacity and it is one of the most prevalent and pervasive negative characteristics of Earth humankind. That is why many souls choose "anger control" lessons in pre-birth agreements, and their learning needs, which are determined by the soul's collective lifetimes, span the anger capacity spectrum.

The capacity for anger, just as with most basic characteristics in Earth humankind, is elastic. If that were not so, "self-control" would be automatic, not the learning experience that life on Earth is all about. The elasticity is what allows the varying degrees of anger that are apparent in a group of people discussing a controversial issue. One person may firmly state his position and another may explode into rage, yet both are reacting to their maximum anger capacity. That is, some people have mastered "anger control" to the point of not feeling that strong emotion, but rather only disappointment or hurt feelings, while those who erupt uncontrollably haven't made a dent in their lesson.

The intensity of anger also is affected by the degree of importance to which the person's vested interests are aroused. When the issue is mildly resented or disagreed with, there is a correspondingly small amount of energy put into anger. The reverse is true when an issue is so deeply ingrained in the psyche that disagreement goes to the very core of the person, such as questioning his or her integrity or attacking convictions of profound importance to an individual, and it is in these situations where the differing anger ranges are especially evident.

Someone whom you may consider to have an irrationally angry disposition may already have progressed from a much more ferocious temperament and need not get stuck even at the improved level. With genuine desire, request for divine help and a strong will, that individual can indeed overcome anger—that may well be the *primary* lesson chosen for this lifetime.

PHOTON BELT

S: The photon belt is hardly controversial—I've never heard any official word on it at all—but what I have heard is confusing and conflicting. Can you give me a definitive answer on what the belt is up to?

MATTHEW: No, Mother, I can't give you a definitive answer. Your scientists can't either, and that is why their information about the photon belt, however limited it is, has widely divergent interpretations. But I can tell you what the belt is and shoot down the theory that you already are in it.

This universal phenomenon is supercharged ions and atomic particles that gathered into a vast band after a supernova exploded billions of years ago in your historical counting. It evolved into an ovoid form, which enabled it to gather orbiting momentum and expand by drawing to itself other cosmic debris until it reached a mass that is detectable many of your calculated light years away. By telescope the belt's leading edge is easily visible as a dense dusky haze, distinctive from the clarity of space beyond its outer fringes.

The full cycle of the belt's irregular movement through space is somewhere between 24,000 and 27,000 years, with its closest point in relation to your planet coming twice during the rotation period. Since its last point nearest Earth was approximately 12,000 years ago, it is natural that a section of your scientific community is speculating about its movement and potential effects on the planet. When they first detected this gigantic belt and were unable to estimate with any degree of precision its size or map its path, they were told by their respective governments not to discuss it outside their few numbers. A benevolent reason for silence could be to avoid frightening everyone about something that may never pose danger, but forcibly suppressing knowledge usually has a sinister purpose. In this case, it is to keep a situation over which there is no human control from motivating people to turn to God directly for "salvation."

Beyond that reason for no official acknowledgment of the belt's existence is the confusion arising from the spectrum of theories. These include a collision that will totally destroy Earth; a proximity that will obliterate all life on it; the belt's gravitational field that will pull Earth into it with unknown effects; the planet's smooth entry into the belt where it will flow for a number of years and then exit; and Earth already is within the belt.

However, bear in mind that the scientists and governments are unaware of Earth's ascension into higher planes of energy—even if the belt's course brings it into proximity with Earth's location the last time it came around, she will be far away from there when it returns. And individuals who have heard via telepathic transmissions that you already are in the belt have heard erroneously because they are not reaching spiritually evolved sources.

Now then, I shall explain why I can shoot down the theory that Earth is within the photon belt. The belt is in a fourth density energy plane. Although "dimension" often is used to mean the same, density is more correct scientifically, and it describes both the level of spiritual awareness, or soul evolvement, and the form, or composition, of energy. Only form applies to the belt. The vast majority of Earth's people are third density beings in both evolvement and form, and to physically survive entry into the belt's fourth density, your bodies would have to be at that same density level. That higher density form is attained by the light changing cellular structure from carbon-based to crystalline, a process that happens due to expanding spiritual awareness. Very few of Earth's total population have completed those cellular changes, and the fact that several billions are alive is incontrovertible evidence that your planet is NOT within the photon belt.

Not that any other evidence is needed, but there is more. The belt is so vast and powerful that entry into it would be unmistakable, possibly with the same cataclysmic destruction as in the past, and nothing even akin to that has occurred. Furthermore, long before that could happen, you would see the belt's unmistakable duskiness without a telescope. And the belt is appropriately named—it is composed of photons. The predominant composition of any celestial body dictates the type of energy prevailing, and on Earth, electrons are predominant. If your planet were within the belt, your source of energy would be photons, not the electrons that supply the electricity for your power generation. Not only do you not have photon-powered appliances, you don't even have any adapters that could let them function.

The belt aside, I hasten to say that light beings in space and on Earth are working hand in hand beaming light to raise consciousness on the planet so spiritual clarity and cellular restructuring can take place. The restructuring raises the body's energy frequency and enables physical survival in the higher densities where Earth is heading, and it also reactivates your innate ability to communicate telepathically.

S: Thank you for explaining all that, Matthew. When

Earth is totally within fourth density where Nirvana already is, will the two worlds unite?

MATTHEW: Nirvana is a discarnate placement where souls live in etheric bodies, and your fourth density bodies still will be physical forms, so I would say that the two worlds will not become one. However, our destination is the same as your own, and as your density is raised from fourth to fifth, Nirvana's will be too.

S: What about civilizations, human or other life forms, elsewhere in the solar system—are all of them included in this package?

MATTHEW: If the populations of those civilizations, some of whom could be called suprahuman because of their great intellectual advancement, are spiritually evolved as well, yes, they will be part of "this package." What an irreverent reference, Mother!

2008:

S: Matthew, it has been about 14 years since you gave me that information about the photon belt. Has anything changed?

MATTHEW: I'm elated to say that it has, Mother! Many, many people have embraced the light during those intervening years and will be accompanying Earth on her journey into the Golden Age! As for the photon belt, it is continuing to roam through the heavens on a course that is taking it farther and farther away from Earth, and I think you should simply chalk up this universal phenomenon as edification in celestial activity.

MIND CONTROL

S: What is mind control by your standards?

MATTHEW: It is the manipulation of a person's mental and physical functioning outside of his true character, desire and motivation. It is achieved through hypnosis with specific suggestions, drugs, sensory deprivation, physical torture, implanted computer-controlled microchips, or whatever combination of those processes and mechanisms achieves the hold of the programming and activates the mind-controlled person.

In a wider sense, promulgation by the media of erroneous information and omission of factual information is a form of mind control, whether or not those who report it know it is false or misleading or that its purpose is to influence people, not to truthfully inform them. In a still different context, mind control is the strategic conditioning of people through governments, schools, churches, military establishments and other agencies and institutions, to believe what they are told without questioning whether it is factual or sound judgment or even rational, and to behave in accordance with that conditioning.

If you could know the massive amount of false information passed on as truth, sometimes innocently but much more often deliberately, you would find it alarming. Consider just the influence the Bible has on lives and remember what I've told you about the current edition's many intentional distortions from the first version, not to mention the huge deviation from the original records.

Developing one's innate capacity to be discerning about all information—knowing what is true and what is not— is essential to consciousness raising and soul evolvement.

S: Matthew, I do try to be discerning, but it's really hard to know what's true and what isn't or what sources to trust.

MATTHEW: Mother, ALWAYS the soul knows the truth! Everyone on Earth needs to get in touch with their souls and trust what resonates, what flows easily within, and not rely on external sources. If you stop trying to analyze, stop the "logical" thinking, thinking, thinking and trust your intuition—the instantaneous reaction to a situation or information that is a message from your soul to your consciousness—you'll receive the answers you need.

S: I'll try harder, dear! Are any of the terrorists in the Middle East operating under mind control?

MATTHEW: Most are not "artificially" mind-controlled because there is no need. Those people are so imbued with hatred stemming from what their people and countries have endured that they don't need external forces to motivate them to act. Not all terrorist activities are committed by those who are blamed for them, but rather are Illuminati plans carried out by CIA "black ops" teams.

But in many seemingly senseless acts of shooting randomly into a crowd, a series of same style killings, and assassinations, mind-controlled individuals are responding to their programming to act upon a specific stimulus. Most were programmed starting at a young age in a special institution where they were confined, and others were inoculated with programmed chips during military service or prison sentences. Sections of the CIA were responsible for this as well as for strategically moving these people around the world to "terrorize" wherever it is politically expedient.

S: Probably you know there's a lot of opposition to chip implants. It's claimed that they're only for beneficial purposes, but can they be programmed to control minds?

MATTHEW: With good reason there is opposition to these chips, Mother! It is true that the claimed benefits could be useful—the tracking of lost children and the elderly with dementia and pets, for instance—but the chips were not designed for that purpose. They are intended to tighten the control by the darkly-influenced people at the top of your world's power ladder by enabling them to track everyone! And absolutely the chips can be programmed in accordance with whatever aims those powers wish to achieve.

Mother, it may seem that I attribute everything in your world that you think of as "evil" to unseen forces that third density brain power cannot comprehend. Nevertheless, it is true that all forms of pain and destruction on Earth are the work of the "dark forces," the vast powerful universal force field composed of the countless negative thought forms that have amassed since the Beginnings. These forms, which have consciousness and substance, attach themselves to energy streamers that, through the universal law of attraction, or "like attracts like," weak-willed individuals pull to themselves by their own thoughts, motives and feelings. When those are rooted in violence, rage, greed, deceit, brutality, corruption, vengeance, prejudice, or desire to control others in any way, "like" thought forms from the dark force field "invade" those individuals who then become the forces' tools, just as puppet masters manipulate their puppets however they wish.

The darkness that originates off-planet is what influences, even controls, the people who in turn devise and implement everything that negatively impacts life in your world, and largely this has been achieved by the massive extent and means of mind control that I described. But I hasten to say that this, like all other darkness in your world, is coming to an end—it literally is "coming to LIGHT."

S: That's the GOOD news in this! Is death a part of pre-birth agreements if it's caused by people who act under mind control, like mass killings or a serial killer?

MATTHEW: Yes, mind control does account for many of those happenings, and often the course of the lives affected is not in accordance with the souls' chosen lessons. However, it is necessary to separate the lesson from the source of the lesson. Even when mind control is a factor, at soul level an individual may willingly be either the perpetrator or the "victim" of a killing IF karmic fulfillment of their soul contracts—each individual's part of the pre-birth agreement that is made by all who want to share the lifetime—requires experiencing either of those roles.

In that case, the perpetrator still may not be a part of the agreement that includes the "victim's" death. The quotation marks are because never is one soul the victim and another the victor. The agreements are based in unconditional love, and the souls who participate fill whatever roles are needed to give all of them the opportunity to balance previous experiencing. So then, when the death-causing event occurs after the "victim's" contract has been completed, the time is the vital factor even though the cause, or the source, may not be the one envisioned when the agreement was made.

It is an entirely different matter when the event causes someone's "premature" death—that is, before the chosen lifetime longevity has been reached and no amended contract was agreed upon by all the principals. That not only prevents completion of the person's contract provisions, it profoundly affects all others in the agreement and many lives far beyond those, and a leveling process must be devised to provide new learning opportunities for every soul affected in any way. When a killing spree results in several "premature" deaths—in homes or schools or colleges, offices, restaurants or stores, wherever the killer is programmed to go—the negative ripple effects are incalculable. If the event occurs prior to completion of the perpetrator's soul contract, it is an interruption in his life, too, because mind-controlled killers are programmed to kill themselves so they cannot be captured alive.

S: Then mind control itself is never part of any pre-birth agreement?

MATTHEW: *NEVER!!!* It absolutely is outside of ALL soul level agreements! Mind control is one of the most pernicious tactics of the dark forces that want to capture all souls in the universe! Consuming all of creation is the ultimate goal of that darkness, which believes its power is greater than Creator's, and that is as much in error as the difference between dark and light! The essence of Creator is pure love, which is the same energy as light and is the most powerful force in the cosmos. Consider that even a spark of light is evident in a dark room, and you can easily see that the limitless and eternal love-light of Creator can only be *and always is victorious.*

But back to mind control. Its prevalence and heinousness is why Creator issued Its decree that released the countless captive souls from the peak dark forces. However, those souls were weakened by eons without free will and many still are under that dark influence, still performing within the intent of the darkness, and that includes controlling minds through all those means I mentioned.

Despite the ever-increasing abundance of light, mind control still is so pervasive that it is a pollutant enveloping the planet. The basest of its motives are behind wars; Satanic torture and human sacrifice; sex slaves, whose minds are "split" and programmed to carry confidential information from one government agent to another; toddlers sold into prostitution; and other perversions of the spirit. Mind control is behind abject poverty and disease and assassinations and ungodly distorted values of world leaders. Even strategic "natural disasters" are technologically contrived by minds that are controlled by the darkness.

Mother, I know I've spoken about this topic with unusual vehemence because it is so important that you know the truth about it, but please do not let that knowledge lead to despair that would not help anyone! Despair leads to fear, a virulent, contagious form of negativity with magnified energy force. Fear is the dark ones' most effective fighting tool as well as their fuel because its energy is incompatible with light. While fear also prevents laughter, joy, clear perceiving, sound judgment, sensible action and peace of heart and mind, its most damaging effect is the blocking of communication between your consciousness and your soul, wherein lies the truth of your inseparable connection with God and all other souls in our universe. So instead of feeling fearful about any information that is deeply disturbing, keep foremost in your thoughts that all forms of darkness will be exposed by the light and all the ills of your world will be healed!

The message I give you from the highest light beings is, BE FEARLESS. Love and care for one another, hold true to your soul's mission by listening to your intuition, your inner voice that is the voice of your soul, and know that your god and goddess selves are eternally in partnership with God and each other.

2008:

S: *Matthew, is mind control still as prevalent as it was all those years ago when you told me about it?*

MATTHEW: This isn't simply a yes or no answer, Mother. Because the higher prevailing frequencies are magnifying all human characteristics and behavior, some individuals, including the very young, have made shocking headlines with their killing sprees. In many instances, they acted under mind control from the strategic programming I told you about, but many individuals are succumbing to their intense indulgence in violent forms of "entertainment" or are reacting irrationally violently to their desires being denied or they're acting out their rage at abusive treatment starting in infancy. As the frequencies have been increasing, so have those kinds of activities.

The bright side of this is, the powerful hold the media once had on minds has greatly diminished. People no longer are unquestioningly trusting mainstream reports of happenings, especially governments' official explanations. While Internet information is polluted with falsehoods, it is a superb source of accurate history and factual current events—one just has to be very discerning as to what is between the two poles, deceit and truth. When the Internet idea was conceived, the Illuminati intended to monopolize its use and disseminate information to further their mass-mind control network, but their plan was short-lived. Lightworkers in increasing numbers have been using this rapid mass communication system to bring forward the truth.

ARMAGEDDON

*S: Matthew, since darkness is coming to an end here,
doesn't that mean that Armageddon won't happen?*

MATTHEW: Armageddon is the term associated
with prophesied events that are being caused by the very
same darkness that developed the Armageddon concept.
Armageddon is ONLY a concept! Like everything else in
this universe, that concept is composed of thought forms.
The source of thought forms is the originator of their
intended effect, and the source of the Armageddon
concept is the dark forces, that powerful universal force
field of negative thought forms.

The promulgation of strategies, which includes
writing the book of Revelations in the Bible, to bring the
concept to fruition has been conducted all along by souls
operating under the influence of the originator—the
dark forces. The purpose is to condition "believers" to put
current happenings into the Armageddon context. The
believers' invested energy in those types of negative
thoughts, especially fear about "the end times," has been
drawing to your planet the kinds of happenings that fit
the doomsday prophecies.

The dark intent of Armageddon is total capitulation
of the light forces on the planet and it will NOT happen!
With the infusion of the Christed light, those negative
thought forms designed to lead to Armageddon are being
transmuted into light and reversing the parade toward
the planetary conquest the dark powers planned. A plan,
or intention, is one thing; being able to carry it to

fruition is quite another!

It is undeniably sad to me that back in antiquity the fall from grace was so pronounced that such darkness was incorporated into the consciousness of humankind. Perhaps when I have progressed more I will understand enough so that what I still see as injustice, tragedy and brutality no longer will be a sad note for me. I do not question any more that Creator's plan is perfect in all its minute details of free will and cause and effect, and I understand that there are growth stages in all happenings for all participants even outside the pre-birth chosen experiences. We are told that The Plan, which is beyond my understanding at this level of soul evolution, was approved by all First Expression fragments and, by inheritance and genetic coding, by all subsequent souls. So in our deepest core, in the seed of the soul, there is approval of all that is happening.

The sooner energy is flowing harmoniously through each soul, the sooner all activity will be blessed with equanimity in spirit, mind and body of All That Is. When all souls have been enlightened to the breadth of godliness in perfection, there will be no more perceived division. There will be the return of all souls into the love and light of God and reintegration with Creator.

2008:

S: Mash, that is one of our earliest conversations. Since then you rose through the ranks of the soul transition team and became its director and later started flying around the universe to assist civilizations upgrade their spirit realms. What I'm wondering is, is the information you give me from your higher vantage point more accurate or comprehensive than when you gave me that message?

MATTHEW: Mother dear soul, of course I've known about your occasional ponderings in this regard, but I have not thought to pop in to talk about it. Indeed, my decade of extensive traveling has given me a far greater awareness of universal happenings and knowledge of our universal family by visiting many diverse civilizations, and my remembering process has revealed an enormous amount of knowledge that *every* soul has as its birthright, as a part of God and Creator.

However, all the information I have transmitted to you during the past fourteen or so years is as accurate as if I had been at this highly evolved station all along. The vast range of information has come from the same reliable sources—God, the souls you call "masters," monitors in Nirvana, light beings from advanced civilizations, and activity in Earth's energy field of potential—and when there is all-around agreement on an issue, I am confident of what I pass on to you.

Mother, I see that your interest has shifted to my information that pertains only to what's happening in your world. Everything I have told you about Earth's true history, what is going on in this unprecedented era, and what to expect in the Golden Age not only is known by intelligent beings throughout this universe, but by *all* of you at soul level!

S: *Then why is there such a great difference in channeled information?*

MATTHEW: There are many reasons, and the most serious by far is that some information is coming from dark sources that claim to be well known highly evolved light beings. The receivers of their messages believe that the dark sources are who they claim to be and they pass on the false, and often fear-filled, information that is transmitted to them.

There are a number of reasons for considerable variances in information from light sources. Whether in spirit worlds or physical civilizations, souls have specialized areas of knowledge, just as you do, and messages from the "specialists" are more accurately detailed and comprehensive than information on the same topic from a "generalist." Souls who are actively involved in a specific kind of assistance to Earth are more knowledgeable of happenings in that area than souls who are aware of it but not participating. One source's perspective and opinion of a situation can differ from another's, just as your perspectives and opinions of the same situation can differ, and those views color the information a source passes to its receiver.

If not all aspects of Earth's energy field of potential are seen by an information source, not all indicators of possible, probable and certain eventualities are considered in the source's conclusions. Information from souls in lower planes of light is not as complete or authentic as information from souls in more highly evolved planes and, however unintentional, information from lower plane sources can be distorted and misleading. And sources transmit information in their personal speaking styles, so semantics can be a cause of confusion

Now then, readers' reception also has a bearing on this situation. If they deem some information to be too "far out" to be believed, they discard what actually is factual. It is possible that messages are not clear to readers and they incorrectly interpret the information. And if messages from one source conflict with messages from another, readers who do not use discernment to determine what is truth and what is not may believe the false information.

Mother, this is why we so often urge everyone to be discerning about information from *all* external sources! It is why we repeatedly have urged that you ask *within* for answers and heed these messages from your soul that reach your consciousness as intuition—that immediate reaction to new information—and as instinct, inspiration, conscience, aspirations. *Always* the messages from your soul contain the truth you are seeking!

PART IX

A SPIRITUAL
RESPONSE TO
TERRORISM

THE RESPONSE

My thoughts as I watched the newscasts September 11, 2001, were about the people who loved those souls whose lives ended so quickly and tragically. Memories of my own experience evoked such powerful empathy for all of the people in shock and grief that I didn't even want to ask Matthew why that horror had happened. His answer couldn't have changed anything.

Then, I received an email from someone who knew about my communication with Matthew. A man representing the group who died in New York City had come to Kalama, as sometimes her patients did as they transitioned between Earth and Nirvana. He said they want to be known as martyrs for peace, not war; that the terror came from within our country, not outside; and they were requesting a "collective voice" through Matthew.

September 16, 2001:

S: Matthew, I just heard from Kalama that a representative of the people who perished in the towers told her they gave you a message. If you have something, I'm sure Jean and Michael will send it out.

MATTHEW: Yes, Mother, I have their message, and I have been asked to speak on behalf of the Council of Nirvana and all other souls in this realm and beyond. We weep. We see the larger picture, but still we weep.

Who could not do that in these days of agonizing shock and sorrow? We urge all souls to feel love, compassion and peace and hold these emotions in your heart—in a moment, your beloved family and friends who so recently came here will speak of this in their own words.

Every one of them is being tended most lovingly, with gentleness and understanding. Many recognize these familiar surroundings from other spirit lifetimes and remember that they knew this was to happen and agreed at soul level to participate. But they, as we, know this cannot comfort the people who love them.

The dark minds behind this seemingly inexplicable agony claim that war will be "justice for those who died." But the war is intended to create even greater negativity in an attempt to extinguish all light on the planet. The perpetrators want you to feel fear and hatred and demand "justice" because they know that only by continuing their cycle of violence can they keep their pernicious hold in this critical time of souls choosing between the light and the darkness. Choose you must, and choose the *LIGHT* you must!

What happened is not a nation against another nation. It is not even a tiny faction of humankind against all other humankind. The root of this madness is a malignant power that most of you don't know exists, but its intentions are so malevolent that Earth herself is weeping. This truth will be revealed in time, but for now, please hold only healing love in your hearts for all life. Let your godself sustain your light so your conscious self won't align with the darkness that wants retaliation, revenge, hatred, more cold-hearted killing.

Let the thousands of lives that left Earth in those fiery moments stand for something besides what the dark ones want. As a collective voice, these recently departed souls are saying:

"Let no more lives be taken. This is the time to keep love above all, for compassion, for bringing healing to the bereaved and injured, for bringing healing to Earth. Please know that the hearts that are hardened into wanting to kill others as their tribute to us, they need light above all. We petition you from the whole of this realm of Heaven to speak of love, of opening eyes to seeing clearly what is happening on Earth, and rising above the tragedy that has been perpetrated by a darkness you cannot even imagine, where your entire world is expendable. We see this from here. We need you to help the myriad light workers by uplifting your hearts and allowing light to come in, by comforting those in fresh sorrow. You must hear our plea. We are working in the light to assist you, and we are forever bonded with you in love."

September 22, 2001:

MATTHEW: The perpetrators are not the individuals who were so quickly accused, but we understand why so many believe the official reports without questioning whether they are complete and accurate or even sound believable. We understand that acceptance instead of analysis is due to the enormity of the planes deliberately hitting their intended targets and the thousands of innocent lives transitioning almost simultaneously from Earth lifetimes. That is too overwhelming to permit mental or emotional margin to see and question the obvious weaknesses in the official story.

S: I have read quite a few Internet reports that blast the official conclusions, so some people definitely are not accepting this as it's being publicly presented. Can you tell me without any wavering at all that the towers would NOT have collapsed if there hadn't been explosives set off?

MATTHEW: Without an iota of wavering, Mother!

S: WHY???

MATTHEW: The destruction had to be in such unthinkable measure that its horror could be filmed—and there's a questionable area, why television cameras were present even in early moments—and aired relentlessly in these days ever since. There had to be such shocking loss of life that it overshadowed speculation about the improbability of the towers collapsing due to the stated reasons, or think too closely about how the planes were taken over and flown unmolested into their targets in supposedly safeguarded air space. Has any irrefutable evidence been presented to prove the official conclusions? No, because there isn't any. Quite the contrary!

The immediate declaration of "This is war!" rather swiftly swerved into the spirit of "patriotism." This serves the real perpetrators' interests because it, too, precludes a public outcry for proof of the official conclusions. The persons they need to accuse as the monstrous evildoers have to be natural suspects, ones who have been indoctrinated in hatred for decades.

The dark minds behind this don't deal with spontaneity. They deal with calculations and strategies developed over decades: If not Plan A, then Plan B; if not the persons originally in charge, then those two or three or four generations later who share the same dark dreams continue to manifest them.

War always was the purpose, and the events of September 11 were to rally unified support for war. The thousands of deaths to gain that support are inconsequential to the dark forces, whose nature is without conscience, honor, compassion, love or empathy. The unconscionably brutal attacks that the darkness manipulated through their willing Earth puppets had to be tied into something that could be presented as so pervasive and so fearsome that the world is united to eliminate "global terrorism." That is exactly what the dark forces had to create so the whole world would be in *FEAR* of it. Light cannot coexist with negativity, and fear is the most powerful of negative emotions, so you can understand why instilling fear throughout the populace is essential to the dark ones' aim of *total planetary conquest.*

But what drives them in their pursuit is a force that is beyond Earth, Mother—that force of darkness to whose influence I have attributed all the ills that have been perpetrated in your world. That vast power is actually a *force field,* or *energy mass,* that so long ago as to be lost to all memory except Creator's, left the light and love *IN* which and *OF* which it was created, and ever since it has been wounded by the absence of light and love. The only way the wound can be healed is by refilling the void with its original ingredients, but if the forces accepted that most powerful of ALL energies, it would have to forfeit its dark powers. It has not been willing to do that, so in its tormented and demented journey throughout all time, it manipulates "puppets" on Earth and elsewhere to create the negativity that sustains it.

The influence of the dark forces is behind the call for

"justice" through more violence and killing. Far from eliminating the roots of "terrorism," those acts refuel the negativity cycle of bloodshed, hatred, tyranny, prejudice, grief and death that insures the continued thriving of darkness. The powers in opposition are the light forces, whose arms and armor are love, compassion and truth.

S: Matthew, do you know how this is going to end?

MATTHEW: God has called in extraterrestrial civilizations to preserve Earth with their technology that can prevent or dilute certain types of destruction and pollution, such as nuclear or biological "weapons of mass destruction" that your government strategically mentions to instill worldwide fear. From our vantage point, the military might and tough rhetoric of these puppets shows the darkness behind them is desperate. Recognizing that it is losing its strongholds on the planet, in its own fear it influenced the ones who planned and implemented September 11's brutal assault on Earth's very spirit.

October 15, 2001:

S: What is happening behind the scenes of the "war on global terror" and the anthrax scare?

MATTHEW: To "scare" everyone is the purpose of the staged incidences of anthrax in your country. Mainstream media, which are controlled by the same dark minds that caused "9/11," are implying that those are the beginning of global biological terrorism. This is a tactic, a ruse, designed to start the fear chain reaction that the dark ones need.

Mother, think about this: First, the media reported the *political fears* that *next* the terrorists will wage biological warfare. And *next*, so quickly as to be amateurishly staged, anthrax turns up and an innocent soul dies. Subsequently powder appears on a floor or a typewriter or in an envelope, and through preconditioning, you instantly suspect it of being anthrax. On the rare occasion it is, but in people's minds now, any powdery substance *anywhere* in any minuscule amount is associated with possible anthrax proliferation globally.

If "death to the infidels" is the aim, since martyrdom is part of that fanaticism, then mass annihilation might suit the "terrorists'" purpose. But to the real perpetrators of this fear tactic, that is *not* acceptable. Anthrax cannot distinguish between the DNA strains of Earth humankind and those of the non-human dark forces that are there disguised in human form, nor between their human operatives and the light workers, so the forces cannot endanger themselves or their cohorts.

More incidents may come, but very strategically selected and only enough to keep the fear alive. *FEAR* is the intent of this, not mass death. Once the fear level reaches saturation, vaccines will be made available so that a plague will not befall those who are protected, or so it will be announced. Without antitoxins for everyone, there could be frenzy to get the small supply available, so fear can be sustained in the people who will not qualify for inoculations.

Mother, it is a diabolical plan indeed, but the intent and results of this anthrax matter are much less harmful long-term than the virtually unquestioned ongoing pollution of your air, ground and water from the "chem-trails," as you call seeding the atmosphere with toxins.

All of these vicious acts are desperate measures to extinguish the increasing light or at least diminish the number of souls whose consciousness is awakening. Fear and frenzy can throw those people back into their cocoon of spiritual slumbering, and that is the purpose behind these acts.

The war is another matter. The intent is to destroy a country, a whole population if necessary, "for the good of the world." Fear about that is intended as well, but the penultimate goal is Iraq's oil and the ultimate goal is world domination.

S: How damaging have the events of the past weeks been to the light forces?

MATTHEW: I cannot say that there has been no damage at all, because the shock, grief, horror and fear that started with the collapsing of the towers has not abated to much extent. However, the additional light that has been pouring in from throughout the galaxy and beyond to shore up the ever-increasing light generated and held fast by light beings of Earth is in greater abundance than before those events.

That is why it is mystifying about the dark forces. Those living on Earth are superior intellectually and technologically to third density humankind, but they are devoid of spirituality. The only light in their souls is that spark of life force from Creator, and they consistently refuse the light that is continually offered. They can't seem to comprehend that with light, they could manifest infinite possibilities. Beings ranging from fourth to seventh density in intellectual, technological and spiritual evolvement also are among you—within, above and on the surface of the planet. They are members of your universal family who have been generating their own light and anchoring vast shafts of light beamed from advanced civilizations off-planet, all of which is aiding Earth's rise out of third density where darkness flourishes.

There has been talk of a "critical mass" that has to be reached before Earth can ascend. It is not the number of souls or a percentage of souls residing on the planet that constitutes critical mass, but rather the degree of light that can be sustained there. That has been reached and surpassed, and Earth's ascension, however misunderstood, is underway. All souls who are receptive to the light are increasing in spiritual clarity as well as changing at cellular level to make the journey physically with Earth.

The souls who refuse the light will not go along. Their physical bodies will die and their lifetime energy registration automatically will take them to other destinations compatible with their free will choices in darkness. Also, many millions of other souls whose lives were made unbearably wretched by actions of the dark souls will leave Earth voluntarily before those days of joyous journeying begin; they will embark upon their own self-selected growth experiencing, perhaps returning for lifetimes in Earth's restored Eden. Many more millions already have left for those reasons.

S: Matthew, can you state unequivocally that if people hold fast to love, compassion, and non-judgment, there is no reason to fear what is ahead?

MATTHEW: Proof far more than my stating so is your assurance despite the headlines and TV newscasts, Mother. That is coming from your soul, which is in touch with the universal mind, the God mind, and *always* is your clearest and purest guidance.

Will there be moments when you cannot see the light in its abundance? Yes, because the "human condition" sometimes lets stress and doubt temporarily dim the awareness of the divinity of each godself. It is especially in those moments that you need to quietly look within, where your soul knows all and you will find the reassurance you are seeking.

If you asked me to give you one thought so profound and inclusive, so uplifting and inspirational that nothing else would be necessary for you to remember, it is this: **Know thy godself.**

2008:

S: *Matthew, this war has gone on for over five years and 9/11 still is being used as the justification for all the deaths and destruction in Iraq and Afghanistan. There's even evidence about what really happened, so why hasn't the truth come out yet?*

MATTHEW: Mother, during this span of time, massive change has been underway, most of it unreported by mainstream media even when the undertakings could be known. Behind the scene, so to speak, the pivotal happening is, that powerful force field of malevolence was driven out of your solar system by the light forces quite some time ago. However, the dark influence on its puppets remains, and the energy of their desires and actions must run its course. However, they know that their former control is in shambles, and they are so overwhelmed by fear that they cannot think or act rationally. They also know that the truth about who planned and implemented that profound terrorist act will be their absolute downfall—that truth is beginning to emerge along with many other truths that have been long-suppressed!

The upheavals in governments and economies herald forthcoming dramatic changes throughout the planet—simply, the "old ways" are broken and new ways are coming in. The dark ones will be replaced by spiritually evolved souls with wisdom and experience to lead your world into an era of peace and harmony among all humankind and Nature. This is more than a hope, it is a promise! The Golden Age, which in linear time the light beings on Earth are creating this moment in union with your space brotherhood, *already exists in the continuum!*

PART X

2012

ESSAY ON 2012

by Matthew

Those who have interpreted the year 2012 as the *beginning* of the end of darkness—never mind the total end of the world!—have misinterpreted its significance. Most simply stated, 2012 heralds Earth's entry into the Golden Age, and between now and then is a time of transition from life as you have known it into life totally in harmony with all of Nature.

Everything in the universe is energy vibrating at one frequency or another, and when Earth was in prime health, in times you know but don't remember, all of her life forms were vibrating harmoniously. When she was near death more than six decades back, there was no harmony whatsoever, no balance of Nature—there was hardly sufficient light to sustain any kind of life, including Earth's own. What is happening now, with the help of stabilizing forces, is the transformation of your world—Earth's rejuvenation and return to balance—reaching completion in 2012.

But that year no longer has the "time absoluteness" it once held in prophecies, and your calendar cannot accurately convey when the major transitional changes will be completed because linear time is disappearing. What you perceive as time passing faster and faster is the effect of the higher energy planes in which you are living now, where everything is accelerating as Earth makes her way into the continuum—or, more accurately, as your consciousness grasps the actuality of timelessness, *the reality of eternity and infinity.* The faster, or more intensely, the light infuses Earth, the more swiftly your "time" passes as she moves still higher into fourth density vibrations. So, just as in this moment your calendar week is passing in less than half the time of a calendar week a dozen or so years ago, 2012 will be coming increasingly more rapidly than your current calendar can indicate.

Now then, why does that year have historic significance universally? It involves celestial orbiting cycles and their influences on your planet as well as life designs made in total clarity by highly evolved beings who planned Higher Universal-MAN with attributes of spirituality and intelligence that far exceed that in today's Earth population. Opportunities to return to higher densities have been offered in prior cycles and missed, and this time when the energetic alignment is again optimal, advanced civilizations are assisting so Earth's desire to rise to her former vibratory level is assured. What happens on Earth affects the universe, so it is of utmost significance to those advanced civilizations that the dark ages on your home planet become reconciled within the light and you knowledgeably take your rightful place among your universal family.

Along the way there will be many profound changes, changes you can't even imagine, that will transform life as you have known it into life in total harmony with all of Nature worldwide and thusly flow out into the universe. Very little of the wondrous world on your horizon will be rooted in your systems to date—that is precisely WHY you are creating your new world! The goddess vibrations that already are showing effects will continue to bless you as individuals and as a civilization.

The negativity that is the root of fear, greed, dishonor and violence will be gone in the Golden Age, and the vibrations of Earth's entirety will be LOVE. Love, which is the same energy as LIGHT but simply expressed differently, is the pure essence of Creator, the ultimate power in the cosmos. This energy is the composition of souls and the key to opening hearts and illumining minds, and it is flowing more abundantly on Earth than ever before. As the darkness continues to fade, love will replace conflict and tyranny with peace and cooperation; love will eliminate the superficial superiority of one group over another; love will enlighten those who regard others as possessions or dispensable and uplift those who have been subjected to living in those conditions. In short, LOVE is the power that is transforming your world.

Although no major strongholds of the darkness will cease abruptly, the transition will be like lightning in comparison to the long ages that violence, inequities, abuses and deceit prevailed. If you could see in parallel motion the pace of the past many centuries, when only intermittent flickers of light broke through the dominant darkness, and the pace of the past few decades of growing light intensity, you would marvel at the swiftness of the changes.

The progressive changes have required and will continue to require the help of extraterrestrials. Almost all of them are unknown to you except as we speak of them and in some cases, their own messages sent forth; yet some of the strongest, most experienced light warriors in this universe are right there among you, working behind the scenes to guide the essential changes so that as many as possible of Earth's residents will accompany her into the higher planes. This is how beloved and significant universally your planet is and how beloved and important YOU are!

In keeping with universal law, it is your heartfelt desire for Earth's well being that is your invitation, your request to those civilizations for their help, but your bewilderment about how to heal the pervasive damage humankind has wrought also is part of their divine authorization to assist. You are in charge, however, because it is your homeland and you chose to be there specifically to participate in this process. That's why millions of you have been inspired to become actively involved or to monetarily support efforts to end violence and environmental destruction.

The first reforms are in governments. Many of the populace who are unaware of the ongoing transformation see governing policies leading to the brink of planetary disaster, and even among lightworkers there are concerns about what will happen in this critical world arena. Not only is it difficult for you to imagine systems dramatically different from what you are accustomed to, but in reforms of the magnitude required, it is realistic to anticipate confusion and foment. Please know that trustworthy souls with spiritual integrity and expertise in the various fields of governing are ready to take the helm and bring order as rapidly as possible as corrupt, tyrannical government leaders are unseated. A great deal of "shuffling" in the United States government will lead to ending its engagement in war and internal and international strife, and the unseating of other self-serving heads of state will end civil wars, genocide and long-standing conflict.

Many wise and able leaders in previous Earth lifetimes chose to return to the planet to complete their groundwork for this unique time at hand, and others are members of your "space family"—many are your ancestors—who volunteered to assist during this transitional period. In no way are they there to take over, but rather they came in response to your thoughts, feelings and actions for peace, fairness and stability in your world. The transformation at hand is *your* desire and soul level vision—if this were not so, it could not happen. Looking even farther ahead, during the past decade or two some souls have come in with the advanced spiritual clarity and ancient wisdom that will naturally put them in leadership roles.

Because money is the basis not only for commerce, but even more so for concentrating power, the need for economic reforms worldwide is as crucial as changes in national leadership. The economy as reported is more myth than actuality. Only a comparative handful of people know how tenuous and corrupt the global economy is or that international trade and the stock markets are manipulated by the Illuminati, a group of darkly-inclined people who have passed their tight global reins from generation to generation.

They have amassed vast fortunes through that control as well as by charging usurious bank loan rates and accruing mammoth amounts from their illegal drugs industry, and they use that money to buy governments; bankrupt countries and exploit their natural resources; keep billions of souls at barely subsistence level; and fund both sides in wars that they precipitate and perpetuate because from wars they derive handsome profits. This cannot continue and it won't. The unconscionably inequitable allocation of money in your world will end. Although I cannot give you finite details of the changeover process, I can give you an overview and assure you that the honest, knowledgeable people who will manage the process will keep disruption at a minimum as they fairly distribute the world's wealth.

The Illuminati's illegally and immorally garnered fortunes will be put into circulation and their exploitation of natural resources worldwide will end. Since that power base is what enabled them to set government and banking policies and own multinational corporations, those corrupt controls also will end. The huge debts of the poorest nations were incurred by their state of desperation, often caused by Illuminati actions and influence; but the loans went to the despots ruling the countries and did not benefit the citizens, so those debts will be annulled and assistance given directly to the people. Many national borders have been set by the victors in war who wanted the natural resources, and that created "have-nots" who formerly were "haves." When the LOVE in souls ends all conflicts, borders no longer will be cause for dispute because all peoples will be "haves."

The coffers of the United States, which is erroneously considered the most fiscally sound nation in the world, have been empty for some time. The national debt, in large part due to the skullduggery of the Illuminati-owned Federal Reserve System and its IRS collection agency, will become manageable when that System is dissolved. The various currencies, especially dollars, have no foundation—daily transactions involving billions of dollars and other currencies are merely information passed from one computer to another and they far exceed the money to back them. The new foundation for currencies will be a return to an old one, where precious metals was a set standard for exchange, and "old fashioned" bartering once again will be an excellent way for nations and communities to conduct some business.

Controlling the flow of money is the last mundane tool the dark ones have and they will keep it within their grasp as long as they can. The "rotten tap root," so to say, has been loosened and the tendrils are breaking, but until all have been eliminated, economic difficulties will affect many lives. Remember, you have the power to create your own abundance through the law of attraction, and sharing your resources is the best way to bring even more abundance into your life.

The basis for much of your current economy will change considerably and employment will change accordingly, but your greater spiritual clarity and usage of brain capacity in the higher frequencies will enable a joyful transition into fields that support cooperation among nations and harmony with Nature. The wanton destruction of your environment through oil and gas extraction, mining, logging and their resultant pollution will cease and all types of toxins in the atmosphere, soil and water will be eliminated. Forests will be restored to the levels required for the balance of Nature, and the need is great as well to preserve and expand habitats where animals have been reduced to countable numbers, just as the oceans must be returned to health so marine life can flourish instead of disappear.

There are plans to achieve those goals as well as keep pristine land areas free of concrete incursions and implement alternative power sources. Technologies known but suppressed and the more advanced technologies that will be introduced by your universal brothers and sisters will clear the pollution and provide renewable energy, new modes of transportation, new types of building materials, and greatly enhanced food production methods. Your hearts will be gladdened at the amazing speed with which these changes will happen!

Natural building products that will come into wide usage along with plants that will be introduced include clay, strong reeds, straw, tropical canes and surface stones, and all will be used in conscious agreement with humankind. While there are countless levels between the lowest and the highest universal intelligence, which you may think of as omniscience, no thing is excluded from the mass consciousness. To be more personal— *indeed, to be more correct*—substitute "soul" for "thing" and you can see the interrelationship of the totality of this universe. The higher the vibrations of any environment, the higher the levels of comprehension of all life within it, thus just as you are expanding in consciousness, so are all the elements of Nature in your world growing in their varying levels of awareness.

The fast-growing food crops, flowers, cotton and other fiber-producing plants, plants with medicinal aspects, canes and grasses, and all kinds of trees will agree to grow as long as needed to meet your require-ments and then transmute their energy into your usage of them. Although much less lumber will be used than currently, the sacred relationship between trees and humankind includes their willingness to be used for decorative parts of building interiors and furniture in the short term, perhaps as long as the next half century. Acknowledgement of all these natural sources' importance and consciousness and gratitude for their willingness to give their lives for your use will become inherent in all peoples. Too, you will come to know and treasure the Devic kingdom that is so closely allied with the beauty and thriving of all that you consider Nature.

The allocation of food and other basic life essentials available in the richer countries will be shared on an equitable basis with the poorer countries until a global production order is achieved. Diets will change from meat and seafood to plants as people learn to respect and honor all animal life. The herds of food animals will decrease through the cessation of breeding and natural transition, and as plants become diet staples, any that were harmfully genetically engineered will shed those properties.

Animals in the wild will instinctively know not to overpopulate and those that are carnivorous will turn to the plant kingdom for sustenance. The albinos being born in several animal species have both spiritual and transitional significance. You associate white with peace, and these rarities that are appearing are symbolic of the coming changes in animal nature that will end the predator-prey food chain and restore the peaceable relationship that once existed among all species, including humankind. The instances of unlikely cross-species friendships and even nurturing of the young from one species by mothers of another are more indications of Earth's return to her original paradise self. Still, an extremely important factor in this is the inspiration in many souls to be advocates for the animal kingdom and alleviate their manmade plight.

The cetaceans' spiritual mission—to embody in huge bulk and inhabit your oceans where they absorb and anchor the light beamed to the planet from distant civilizations—soon will have been fulfilled. These whale and dolphin souls, which species-wide are the most highly evolved spiritually and intellectually on your planet, will soar to their original light stations when they leave physically, but they will continue to grace your planet with their love energy.

What are commonly known as "global warming" and

"El Niño" are part of Earth's natural processes to return
to her original moderate climate everywhere. While she
is achieving this, glaciers will melt, the vast deserts will
become arable, rain forests will flourish, and variations
in temperatures will markedly decrease—ultimately,
everyplace in your world will be comfortably habitable.
Peoples now living in the coldest or the hottest climes
will adapt, but it is unavoidable that the few animal
species in the polar regions will disappear and some that
live on the fringes will survive by migrating; the affected
species instinctively will know not to reproduce or when
to move.

Contrary to current count and certainly population
projections, your numbers are decreasing and the birth
rate will continue to drop but not precipitously. The
balance of Nature no longer will require pestilence, so no
disease-causing or transmitting factors will be present,
and the common use of toxic chemicals and prescription
drugs will cease. Medical treatments will drastically
change until there no longer is any need for therapies
because bodies, which will have a greatly longer lifetime,
will become free of all forms of dis-ease. New educational
systems and resource materials will reflect factual
universal and planetary history, and true spirituality
will replace religions in accordance with the truths that
will be revealed.

Those are some of the most significant changes
underway and ahead, and all will have trickle-down
effects that will permeate and uplift every facet of life on
Earth. The Golden Age—the "second edition" of the
Garden of Eden—will radiate the love, harmony, serenity
and beauty of spirit that you, in your remembered
awareness of being god and goddess selves, ARE.

Now I shall tell you some of the more "down-to-

Earth" features that you can anticipate in that beauteous world. City life will be much more fulfilling for the spirit than it is today due to the demolishing of substandard buildings and restoration of once fine buildings that fell into decay; and the addition of many small parks and colorful playgrounds, vegetable and flower gardens, neighborhood libraries, concerts, museums and galleries with locally produced art forms. There will be entertainment and recreational centers for all ages and interests; and animals, even those you now consider wild, will roam freely among all the peoples.

New transportation modes and a much fairer distribution of wealth will enable city dwellers to frequent the countryside, where a booming business will be "bed-and-breakfast" inns to accommodate the growing desire for those oases of respite from routine activity, and to travel to distant places as well. Still, millions now living in cities may prefer to move to the solitude and restorative energy of familiar rural, forested areas. And, like a new wave of pioneers, some of you will be motivated to relocate to currently uninhabitable places when those start flourishing and beckon the adventuresome, while other souls will choose to live in houseboats on the calm, restful seas.

Architecture will be limited only by imagination and choices, but no building will be ugly or inadequate for its purpose. Geodesic domes will be popular as will fanciful building designs that reflect the lightheartedness that so long has been denied the majority of Earth's peoples. Current and new technologies will produce construction materials similar in strength and appearance to today's concrete, steel, rigid and flexible plastics, and those along with natural products and quality simulations of fine woods will be widely used. So will glass, which will be altered from its present composition, because you will desire to live closer with Nature even when you are indoors.

By unified intent, no litter or eyesore of any kind will exist anywhere. Wherever you live or travel, you will not want the vista marred by the utility poles that now are necessary blights on landscapes. The poles will be removed and where conduits are required, they will be underground; and other energy sources will be direct, without any need for connecting wires. Although telepathy will become a common form of communication, voice-to-voice communion across the miles will be as important as now, but the harmful aspects of the wireless methods you are using will be gone. Expanses of concrete gradually will be removed too, as new transportation modes will change the need for current fuels and highways.

All unjust laws and policies will be struck down and education worldwide will accurately reflect the universal truths. The writing, printing and distribution of textbooks will be done expeditiously in conjunction with computerized lessons, and the souls who are innately prepared to teach will step up to this mission they had chosen.

These and other marvelous lifestyle differences awaiting you are indeed gargantuan changes from life in this moment, yet the greatest transformation you will experience is in humankind, where love and higher consciousness are REcreating "miracles." Like souls on Earth and in Nirvana once again going back and forth between these physical and spirit worlds, travel that was commonplace until third density limitations closed minds to this possibility. Like your transcendence from believing you are lone individuals to knowing your inseparability from all life in this universe, and embracing each other as well as members of extraterrestrial civilizations as the brothers and sisters you all are. Like life without anxiety or conflict as peoples of all countries and cultures are harmonious, cooperative, helpful, kind, high-spirited and delightfully good-natured.

Now I must tell you as well that the transition from this day to that world will continue to present challenges. To say otherwise would be neither truthful nor prudent as your expectations would not be met, and instead of successfully dealing with challenges—which you are well prepared to do with wisdom and strength of spirit and character or you wouldn't have chosen and been selected to participate!—you could become discouraged as Earth continues apace on her ascension journey

Wars and other violence, injustices, deception and corruption will continue until that energy set in motion is played out. Although the dark forces—the vast force field of negative thought forms—has left this part of the galaxy, tentacles of that energetic influence remain and are making last ditch efforts to control the most vulnerable souls as well as attack those with the brightest light.

The puppets of the dark forces are those who desire to control the world, who are greedy, ruthless, violent and deceptive, and their most effective tool to achieve and maintain their power and vast fortunes is *fear*. The energy of fear, which is incompatible with the energy of light, forms a barrier between light and consciousness and renders fearful people incapable of opening their minds to enlightenment, prevents sound reason and judgment, and stifles the flow of love for and from others. *When one lives in the light, there is nothing to fear and love flows in abundance!*

The higher frequencies now on the planet are magnifying all human characteristics, and those that are darkly-inclined are showing this intensification through increasing hostility, greed, violence and apathy toward those who are suffering and in desperate need. So, while not all of the dark skirmishes are past, we urge you to be encouraged by each that arises—it means that the vanquishing of the darkness is that much nearer. Rejoice in knowing that its momentum is close to the point of exhaustion because all of you who are living your light are helping to speed it to conclusion.

Prior to peace and harmony prevailing throughout Earth, many, many souls will leave due to the same causes as now—disease, starvation, injuries in wars and other types of violence, geophysical events—so the population will continue to decrease from those means. As sorrowful as these deaths may seem, the adversity that the souls experience beyond their pre-birth agreements gives them leaps forward in soul growth. They will greet their return to Nirvana knowing that if they choose another Earth lifetime, it will be in the splendor and glory of a revitalized world and the abiding love among its inhabitants.

Geophysical events will continue as Earth's natural and necessary cleansing process. The blatant disregard for human and animal life for millennia past—and still happening on a lamentable scale—caused a massive amount of negativity to accumulate. Although this has been greatly reduced via geophysical events, its remnants and what is being generated anew must be released. It matters not whether this is by natural or manmade occurrences—the ridding of that negativity is what is important.

The effects of these events, which will lessen in frequency and severity as Earth keeps ascending, are being diminished to the greatest extent possible by members of your universal family. Their technology cannot prevent all deaths and damage, but it is limiting the death toll and property destruction by leveling out over a wide area the energy releases via earthquakes and volcanic eruptions and by steering the strongest storms to less populated areas.

The record high and low temperatures, droughts and flooding that are part of Earth's transition to her original moderate climate globally will present hardships for a while longer. Gradually some sea level coastlines will become submerged; this need not present anxiety as there will be protective and compensatory measures for any inhabitants of those areas.

We are aware of the speculation that Atlantis and Lemuria may rise, but this will not happen. Those large land masses served their civilizations during that era on Earth, but their return is not needed; however, some souls living then have come back to assist in the ongoing consciousness-raising and spiritual renewal within today's populace.

That religions are teaching the "word of God" will be shown in the fullness of the deception that spawned that falsehood, and among the challenges you will encounter are the many individuals who will not believe the truths that will be revealed. Some will do battle, convinced that it is their divine right and duty to defeat the Anti-Christ or the "infidels" through bloodshed. You will witness shock, confusion, anger, disillusionment, and yes, very likely fear—the deceivers who made a vengeful God have masterfully perpetuated that lie for eons—of people whose minds are not totally closed to the revelations.

Provide a compassionate safe haven for their questioning and rely on your intuition for the best responses—they will be there when you need them.

However, it is not your responsibility to convince them that the foundation of their beliefs—maybe even their very life purpose—is a lie. Rejoice, just as we shall, when your efforts succeed, but please do not feel despondent when they don't. The resistant souls, like all others in the universe, will continue their evolutionary pathways wherever their needs shall best be served, and the eternal and infinite love of Source will undergird their way.

In summary we say to you, our beloved Earth family, know with your entire being that the world of love, peace and harmony you have been co-creating is close at hand. Remembering that you chose to be exactly where you are right now so you could participate in this unprecedented time in the universe will let your hearts be light-filled and your journey a triumphant adventure. Myriad light beings are with you every instant, enfolding you with the love and protection of the Christed light as you usher in Earth's long awaited "2012" Golden Age.

GLOSSARY

Akashic Records. Universal recording and storage system of all souls' experiencing in all lifetimes

Angelic realms. Placements of pure love and light close to Creator

Angels. Collective beings of light manifested by archangels in co-creation with Creator

Archangels. First beings created by Creator

Aspect. Each part of a cumulative soul; also called personage, soul fragment, God spark

Aura. Light within a life form reflected through and surrounding the physical body

Balance. Goal and epitome of all experiencing

Christ. State of being one with God

Christed light. Manifestation of Creator's love; the most powerful force in the cosmos, constantly available to all beings for soul evolvement and protection from dark forces

Co-creation. Process or product of souls using Creator's energy to manifest their ideas

Continuum. The timeless universal vastness where linear time's past, present and future are a series of simultaneous events in the multiple lifetimes of souls

Cosmos. The total of Creation, all the universes; sometimes used interchangeably with "universe" in reference to our universe

Creator/Creation, Creator. Supreme Being of the cosmos; also referred to as Totality, Oneness, All That Is, I AM, Source; sometimes used interchangeably with God to denote the Supreme Being of our universe

Creator mind. All knowledge in the cosmos; the total of all thought forms; also called God mind, universal mind, mass consciousness

Cumulative soul. Ever-expanding composite of all experiencing in all lifetimes of its individual personages; may be called oversoul or parent soul

Darkness, dark energies, dark forces. Powers originating in deepest antiquity whose experiencing choices eventually eliminated all light except a spark at soul level; foes of light beings and of the light itself; evil

Density. Soul evolution status, ranging from the pure light and love of Creator to total spiritual darkness; the form, or composition of anything manifested, including physical and celestial bodies

Duality. Opposing attitudes and characteristics inherent in humankind

Energy. Indestructible basis of all life throughout the cosmos

Energy attachments. Positive or negative results or interpretations given effects of energy motion

Etheric body. Body used by souls in spirit realms; integral part of the physical body

Extraterrestrial. Any place beyond Earth; non-Earth civilizations

First Expression. Creator's first dividing of Itself; the creation of the highest angelic (Christed) realm; the "Big Bang"

Fragmentation. Creator dividing Itself into parts that share Its powers proportionally; a soul dividing into interconnected parts for independent experiencing

Free spirit. Lifetime of a soul without an etheric or astral body; and/or conscious communion with God and awareness of pre-birth agreement

Free will. Each soul's Creator-given right to choose what to manifest

God. One name given the Supreme Being of our universe, and as such, possessing all power, wisdom and knowledge of Creator

God spark. Aspect of God within soul essence of every individual; also known as god-self, higher self, inner voice

Gods, goddesses. Generic terms for the rulers of the universes; the highest spirit beings and mortals in the universes

Guardian angel. Primary celestial helper assigned to each person for spiritual guidance and physical protection

Karma. Cause and effect of a soul exercising free will; basis for selecting lifetime experiencing

Lifeprint. A soul's file in the Akashic Records; complete accounting of a soul's thoughts, feelings, actions and their consequences during all lifetimes

Light. Creator's wisdom, love and the power of love manifested in energy form

Lost souls. Souls whose free will choices energetically led to their being reabsorbed by Creator

Manifesting. Process of co-creating with Creator; the inherent ability and indivisible part of free will

Mission. Primary purpose of each lifetime, selected for spiritual growth by the soul prior to birth of its personage

Negativity. Destructive force initiated and expanded by negative thought forms

Nirvana. Proper name of the spirit world we call Heaven

Personage. Independent and inviolate essence of a soul experiencing an incarnate lifetime

Placement. Any realm composed of various related areas for specific experiencing

Planetary cleansing. Earth's preservation of her

planetary body through natural forces to dispel
accumulated negativity

Prayer. Direct communion with God through thoughts
and feelings

Pre-birth agreement. Agreement made prior to
incarnation by all primary souls who want to share
the lifetime; agreements are made in unconditional
love and designed with opportunities for all participants to evolve spiritually

Reabsorption. Act of Creator drawing back into Itself
the lost souls

Reincarnation. Return to a physical life after a life in
spirit

Reintegration. Through spiritual evolvement, the
return of all souls to God, then to Creator

Root soul. A soul created in The Beginnings; the originator
of countless soul fragments throughout all time

Shan, Terra, Gaia. Other names for planet Earth

Soul. A part of God, formed by Creator's energy; spiritual
life force; inviolate essence of each individual's
inextricable connection with all other life forms
throughout the cosmos

Soul fragment/spark, sparklet, subsparklet. A
soul's successive divisions for individual experiencing
in any life form; also called God fragment, God spark,
or simply soul

Soul lineage. All the personages of a soul

Soul transference. Process whereby a soul agrees to
leave its physical body and another soul agrees to
enter; also known as a "walk-in"

Spirit guides. Discarnate souls not from angelic realms

Thought forms. Indelible, indestructible energy
substances produced by mental processes of all souls
from The Beginnings; the stuff of universal

knowledge

Transition. Upon death of the physical body, the soul's lightning-fast passage in etheric body to Nirvana

Universal laws. Parameters within which all souls experience and to which all are subject; also called laws of God, laws of nature

Universal knowledge, universal mind. All knowledge in the universe; the total of all thought forms, available for accessing by any soul; may be called God mind, Creator mind, mass consciousness, "universal soup"

Universe. One of several such placements of incalculable size manifested by Creator and the god or goddess Creator selected to rule over each universe

OTHER MATTHEW BOOKS

Matthew, Tell Me about Heaven
A Firsthand Description of the Afterlife

Life in the spirit world we call Heaven   **Matthew Ward**
is active, vibrant and temporary. Matthew   **1962-1980**
describes the reception of arriving souls,
environment, relationships, communication, animals, reunions,
nourishment, recreation, education, cultural resources,
employment, pre-birth agreements, karma, past-life reviews,
and preparation for our next physical lifetime.

Illuminations for a New Era
Understanding These Turbulent Times

God explains who He is, who we are, and the purpose of
our multiple lifetimes; and extraterrestrial beings help us
understand our place in the universal family. Read about
Earth's ascension progress, how our thoughts create our reality, the healing power of love-light, the destructiveness of fear,
and the reasons for the war in Iraq.

Voices of the Universe
Your Voice Affects the Universe: Let It Be with LOVE

The voices of God, Earth souls in spirit, members of our
universal family and some of our own show the interconnectedness of All. Synchronicity in life experiences and the influence
of the Illuminati give insight into this unprecedented time on
our planet as Earth is restored to her Eden self, the Golden
Age, and our roles in this transformation.

Earth's Golden Age—Life beyond 2012

What is the planet's ascension all about? How does it affect us? Why is 2012 a pivotal year? If there are spiritually, intellectually and technologically advanced civilizations, who are they? Where are they? How are they helping us? Who will enter the Golden Age with Earth? What will life be like then? This book has the answers.

Amusing to Profound
My Conversations with Animals I and II
Suzanne Ward

What the animals in this book talk about shows that the range and depth of intelligence, emotions and comprehension in Earth's animal kingdom far exceeds what usually is attributed to any life except human. These animals' comments—at times, with astounding knowledge and perception—will evoke smiles, amazement, and maybe heartwarming memories or a tear or two.

Order these books at www.matthewbooks.com or your favorite local or on-line bookstore.

MESSAGES
Matthew's messages from December 2003 to date are posted on **www.matthewbooks.com**. Topics include current events in a universal context, the ongoing spiritual renewal and world transformation, effects of planetary cleansing and Earth's ascension into higher vibrations, and what we can expect during the transitional period through 2012 and beyond, the era of the Golden Age. Translations of the messages into 23 languages are posted at **www.galacticchannelings.com**.